How to
think
LIKE
MANDELA

DANIEL SMITH

Michael O'Mara Books Limited

In loving memory of Zöe Anne Wright (Née Lloyd)
7 June 1975 – 31 December 2013
(How to Think Like Zöe: try to be happy in all that you do; don't
work too hard; spend time with friends and family; don't grumble
too much; have an adventure every day; be kind; volunteer)

First published in Great Britain in 2014 by
Michael O'Mara Books Limited
9 Lion Yard
Tremadoc Road
London SW4 7NQ

A CIP catalogue record for this book is available from the British Library.

Papers used by Michael O'Mara Books Limited are natural, recyclable
products made from wood grown in sustainable forests. The manufacturing
processes conform to the environmental regulations of the country of origin.

ISBN: 978-1-78243-214-2 in hardback print format
ISBN: 978-1-78243-241-8 in paperback print format

1 2 3 4 5 6 7 8 9 10

www.mombooks.com

Designed and typeset by Envy Design Ltd

Printed and bound by CPI Group (UK) Ltd, Croydon CR0 4YY

How to *think* LIKE MANDELA

Contents

Introduction

'He is at the epicentre of our time, ours in
South Africa, and yours, wherever you are.'

NOBEL LAUREATE NADINE GORDIMER

The first draft of this book was liberally sprinkled with verbs in the present tense. That is to say, as I was writing it, Madiba – though old and in ailing health – was still very much *with us*. By some sad chance, I finished typing the last few words on the evening of 5 December 2013. I promptly made what I thought would be a celebratory cup of tea, switching on the radio as the kettle boiled. Of course, the first thing I would hear was a newscaster mournfully reporting that Mandela had died. That a few minutes earlier I had been writing about him in the present tense only made the news more poignant for me.

In the days that followed, the great and the good came forward to pay their tributes. Some seemed to grow in stature, rising to the occasion with dignity and insight;

others merely seemed smaller in Mandela's shadow. But it was a few words spoken to me by a colleague the day after Madiba's death that stuck in my memory. 'If you had asked me yesterday morning to name the world's greatest living human,' he said, 'I could have done it. Ask me today and I just don't know.' That, I think, speaks volumes about Mandela's role in our collective history.

He undoubtedly claims a place in that select group of those who may legitimately be called giants of the twentieth century. After years of bitter struggle that saw South Africa freed from the bondage of apartheid, he came to be acknowledged not only in his own country but around the world as a unifying force for good. Almost uniquely, he was a figure as popular with the poorest resident of the most disadvantaged neighbourhood in Johannesburg as with the politicians and celebrities who clamoured to be photographed beside him.

It is testament to his enduring importance that commentators spent the months leading up to his death asking whether South Africa could manage without him. Quite simply, of course it will, and that it is equipped to do so – however imperfectly – is surely his greatest legacy. Yet few can doubt that the Rainbow Nation is diminished by his absence.

If the end of white rule in South Africa came almost as suddenly and dramatically as the collapse of communism in Europe – events that were nearly contemporaneous – it should not hide the fact that Mandela led a movement whose members had made devastating sacrifices for decades. He himself emerged from almost thirty years in prison to oversee the final negotiations that brought multiracial democracy to his country for the first time. More significantly, perhaps, was that the final transition took place in relative peace.

In 1994, Mandela became President of the nation and leader of a government dominated by his African National Congress, an organization that until shortly before had been treated by the apartheid regime as a terrorist organization. During his tenure, he re-established South Africa on the global stage after many years of international isolation. Domestically, he kept the whole show on the road at a time when a lesser figure might have lost control. There were, of course, problems, many of which continue today. Vast income inequality means that South Africa remains a nation of haves and have-nots, while crime and HIV/AIDS blight millions of lives. But through it all, both the white and black populations have remained overwhelmingly committed to the ideal of a society where an individual's fate is not dependent upon the colour of their skin.

Faced with the most precarious of tightropes, Mandela showed assured fleet-footedness until giving up the presidency in 1999. Not for him the urge to keep a steely grip on power, a temptation to which so many of Africa's post-colonial leaders have succumbed. Instead he ceded power to the next generation, aware that the nation's future should not be tied up in a single individual. Removing himself from front-line politics, he evolved into an elder statesman who was a stabilising force at home and a spokesman for peace and justice internationally.

In fact, he became for millions across the globe nothing less than an icon. A freedom fighter who, it sometimes seemed, had brought down a corrupt and bankrupt system virtually singlehandedly. In the years after 1990, he developed an outward aura of almost superhuman tranquillity. He became the epitome of forgiveness and inner calm, a symbol of equanimity. Those who knew him speak of his remarkable ability to be still. He never crafted a halo for himself but he had one thrust upon him by a world hungry for heroes in an age when they are in short supply.

But Mandela himself was the first to admit that he was far from angelic. He was, as we all are, much more complex than that. Of course, until recent decades he was not always such a warmly-received figure anyway. Driven by grand goals, he could be ruthlessly pragmatic in their pursuit. For a large part of his life he was regarded, even by some of those who came to fete him, not so much as a freedom fighter but as a terrorist. It is true that he came to believe that civil protest of the type favoured by Gandhi in India was inadequate for South Africa, and eventually condoned and actively pursued armed struggle. Extraordinarily, it was only in 2008 that Mandela was finally removed from the US's terrorism watch list. Furthermore, his political leanings were instinctively to the left, which did not always endear him to leaders in the West engaged in the Cold War. His personal life, too, was not without its complications, including two marriages that ended in messy divorce.

Though Mandela was treated as a figure virtually beyond reproach in the years after his release from prison, the truth of the man was considerably more nuanced. That does not imply a criticism. Simply, it acknowledges that alongside his myriad qualities, skills and talents, he had his foibles and faults as well. He was not a saint or angel after all, but a human being just like you and me, though one who gave up much to cement his place in history. This book will, I hope, cast a light on some of the ideas, attitudes and motivations that moulded one of the great figures of our age.

Landmarks in a Remarkable Life

1918   Rolihlahla Dalibhunga Mandela is born on 18 July in the Transkei, in the Eastern Cape of South Africa, to Gadla Mphakanyiswa and Nonqaphi Nosekeni.

1920   The Mandela family moves to the village of Qunu, to where Nelson will return in his retirement.

1925   Mandela begins his schooling, the first of his family to attend. His teacher gives him the name Nelson.

1927   Gadla Mphakanyiswa dies. Mandela is made the ward of Jongintaba Dalindyebo, acting Thembu regent, and is brought up in the royal household.

1939   Mandela enrols at Fort Hare University to train as a civil servant.

1940   He is dismissed from Fort Hare without graduating for his role in a protest against the university authorities.

1941   Faced with an arranged marriage, Mandela

flees to Johannesburg, where he is befriended by Walter Sisulu and begins working for a legal firm.

1942   Mandela becomes involved with the African National Congress (ANC).

1943   He enrols to study law at Witwatersrand University

1944   With Oliver Tambo and Walter Sisulu, he joins the ANC and co-founds the ANC Youth League (ANCYL). He also marries Evelyn Mase.

1945   Evelyn gives birth to a son, Madiba Thembekile.

1947   Mandela is elected to Transvaal's provincial ANC executive. Evelyn gives birth to a daughter, Makaziwe, who dies aged nine months.

1948   The National Party is voted into power and implements its programme of apartheid.

1949   The ANCYL responds with a Program of Action, a campaign of passive resistance incorporating mass strikes, boycotts and other protests.

1950   Mandela joins the ANC National Executive and assumes the presidency of the ANCYL. Evelyn gives birth to a son, Makgatho.

1952   Mandela and Oliver Tambo establish the first black law firm. The ANC launches the non-violent Defiance Campaign. Mandela is convicted of violating the Suppression of Communism Act and given a suspended sentence. He is also banned from attending public meetings. Nonetheless, he is elected Deputy President of the ANC and begins drawing up plans for underground campaigns.

1954   Evelyn gives birth to a daughter, Pumla Makaziwe (Maki).

1955   The ANC establishes the Congress of the People, an organization representing all races to evolve a set of core principles for a new South Africa. These principles are brought together in the 'Freedom Charter'.

1956   In December, Mandela and some 150 others are arrested. Their subsequent trial for high treason will last several years.

1957   Mandela and Evelyn divorce.

1958   Mandela marries Winnie Madikizela.

1959   The Pan African Congress splits from the ANC. Parliament establishes a number of 'tribal homelands' and begins the enforced resettlement of blacks, a move vehemently opposed by the ANC. Winnie gives birth to a daughter, Zenani.

1960   Winnie gives birth to a daughter, Zindziswa (Zindzi). In March, the Sharpeville massacre focuses international attention on the apartheid regime.

1961   Mandela and his co-defendants are acquitted in the so-called 'Treason Trial'. He subsequently goes underground and becomes Commander-in-Chief of Umkhonto we Sizwe (MK), the ANC's newly established armed wing.

1962   Having returned from intelligence-gathering

tours of Europe and Africa, Mandela is convicted of leaving the country without permission and inciting workers' strikes. He is convicted to five years in prison.

1963   Following a raid on an ANC building in Rivonia, Mandela is one of several ANC leaders charged with attempting to violently overthrow the government.

1964   In April, Mandela delivers his landmark Rivonia address from the dock. He is found guilty as charged, sentenced to life in prison and sent to Robben Island.

1968   Mandela's mother dies. He is refused permission to attend the funeral.

1969   Mandela's eldest son, Thembi, is killed in a car crash. Again, the prison authorities refuse him permission to attend the funeral.

1974–5   Mandela works on his biography in secret.

1976   He rejects a conditional reduction of his sentence.

1980   The exiled Oliver Tambo spearheads the ANC's 'Release Mandela' campaign.

1982   Mandela is transferred from Robben Island to the mainland Pollsmoor Prison.

1983–4   Violence spreads from the black townships of Johannesburg in protest at rent increases and the failure of the government to grant blacks increased representation in parliament. Strikes and boycotts are supplemented by increased activity from MK guerrillas.

1985   Mandela rejects Prime Minister P. W. Botha's offer of freedom in return for a renunciation of violence as a state of emergency is declared. However, informal channels of contact between Mandela and the government open up.

1986   Mandela begins talks with Prime Minister P. W. Botha but does not immediately tell his ANC colleagues. Winnie, meanwhile, draws international attention when she makes a speech that is widely interpreted as a call to violence.

1987   News of Mandela's private talks with the government spreads. Reactions from within the ANC range from strong support to accusations of betrayal.

1988   Mandela is transferred to Victor Verster Prison after a bout of tuberculosis. In December, four youths are abducted and beaten by members of the Mandela United Football Club (Winnie Mandela's bodyguards). One of them, fourteen-year-old Stompie Seipei, is killed.

1989   Botha is succeeded as Prime Minister by F.W. de Klerk. Talks with Mandela continue and de Klerk begins to free political prisoners and accepts the principle of 'power sharing'.

1990   On 2 February de Klerk lifts the bans on the ANC. Nine days later Mandela is freed from prison. He becomes Deputy President of the ANC. Talks between the ANC and the National Party begin on the future of South

Africa. Mandela and de Klerk continue private discussions against the background of an upsurge in violence in many black townships, especially in Natal.

1991   Winnie Mandela is convicted for her role in the 1988 kidnappings that culminated in the death of Stompie Seipei. Her sentence of six years in prison is reduced to a suspended sentence and fine on appeal. Her husband, meanwhile, is elected ANC President.

1992   Mandela and Winnie announce their separation. There is tension between Mandela and de Klerk as the former implicates the police in the rising tide of violence sweeping the country and the ANC orchestrates a general strike. In September, Mandela and de Klerk sign a Record of Understanding to investigate the activities of the police and to establish an elected constitutional assembly to prepare a new national constitution.

1993   Mandela appeals for calm in the aftermath of the murder of prominent ANC figure Chris Hani on 10 April by a white extremist. Mandela and de Klerk are jointly awarded the Nobel Peace Prize.

1994   The ANC wins a majority in the country's first democratic, multi-racial general election. On 10 May, Mandela is inaugurated as President of South Africa.

1995   The Nelson Mandela Children's Fund is established.

1996   Mandela and Winnie divorce. The Truth and Reconciliation Commission is inaugurated.

1998   On July 18, his eightieth birthday, Mandela marries Graça Machel.

1999   The ANC wins the general election. The presidency passes from Mandela to Thabo Mbeki. The Nelson Mandela Foundation is established.

2000   Mandela announces that he is retiring from public life.

2001   He is diagnosed with prostate cancer.

2002   The Mandela Rhodes Foundation is established.

2003   Mandela speaks out against the US-led war in Iraq.

2004   Mandela 'retires from retirement' as his health declines.

2005   Mandela's son by Evelyn, Makgatho, dies from AIDS.

2007   A statue of Mandela in unveiled in Parliament Square, London. Meanwhile, the Mandela-inspired Elders group is established.

2009   The UN marks the first International Nelson Mandela Day on 18 July, his birthday.

2013   Mandela spends long periods in hospital as his health declines. He dies on 5 December, aged ninety-five, at his home in Houghton, Johannesburg, surrounded by his family.

Believe You Can Make a Mark

'By ancestry, I was born to rule… my real vocation
was to be a servant of the people.'

NELSON MANDELA, 2003

When Nelson Mandela was born there was little to suggest that he was destined to become one of the most important figures in the global politics of his time. However, he never lacked for self-confidence, always possessing a deep-rooted belief that he was worth as much as any other human. This is not to say that he thought there were not people who were 'better' than himself – whether that meant wiser, intellectually smarter, physically superior or gifted in some other way. Instead, it was a reflection of Mandela's fundamental faith in meritocracy; the idea that no individual should be judged on the chance circumstances of their birth but on their character and actions instead.

That a black child in early twentieth-century South Africa would be so imbued with the ideals of meritocracy was something of a rarity, given that the society was one where ethnic background had a decisive impact on your life prospects. Nonetheless, at a time when millions had their lives utterly blighted purely because of the colour of their skin, Mandela managed to remain faithful to the notion that all humans enter the world as equals.

He was born on 18 July 1918 in Mvezo, a small

village in Transkei in the eastern part of what is now the Eastern Cape province. By the time of his birth, the majority black population had for centuries been subjugated by an uneasy mix of Dutch and British settlers. An example of their institutionalised mistreatment was the Native's Land Act of 1913. This piece of legislation regulated the black ownership of land at a time when only about seven per cent of the nation's territory was in their ownership, despite the fact they comprised over two-thirds of the population.

It is conceivable that if Mandela had been born into poverty in a backwater township, the world may have been deprived of his influence. Instead, he was brought up in a family descended from Thembu royalty (the Thembu being one of twelve Xhosa-speaking chieftaincies). In accordance with the rules of patrimonial descent that operated among the chieftaincies, Mandela's father, Gadla Mphakanyiswa, was ruled out from holding the highest offices but was a local chief and served as an advisor to the Thembu king. As the son of his father's third wife, Mandela himself would have expected a similar role in adulthood.

So while Mandela's quote at the beginning of this section (which he made in 2003) could be open to misinterpretation, he was nevertheless born into an elite. When he was still very young, his father was found guilty of insubordination to a local magistrate and lost both his title and much of his wealth. Nonetheless, the young Mandela would have continued to receive a certain level of deference from his contemporaries and got to see at close hand how traditional African power structures operated.

He held a prominent role within his immediate family unit too, being the first son of his mother, Nonqaphi Nosekeni, and older brother to three full sisters (his father had a total of thirteen children, so there were several half-brothers and sisters too). In a strongly patriarchal society, he would have felt the burden of responsibility even more acutely with the death of his father in 1927. It was an early lesson in how to deal with personal loss and tragedy – a tough but valuable lesson for a man who would experience both with dispiriting regularity throughout his life.

Following his father's passing, he came under the direct patronage of the Thembu regent, Jongintaba Dalindyebo. He moved to the regent's extensive personal compound, known as the 'Great Place', where he received yet more exposure to the mechanisms of tribal government. He saw up close the all-male, open air tribal meetings at which a range of opinions on disparate matters were asked for and offered until a plan of action was broadly agreed upon. This was consensual democracy in action and it would inform Mandela's entire adult career. In a speech he made shortly after his release from prison in 1990 he reflected on some of the lessons he had learned in this period:

In our custom and history, the chief is the mouth-piece of his people. He must listen to the complaints of his people. He is the custodian of their hopes and desires. And if any chief decides to be a tyrant, to take decisions for his people, he will come to a tragic end in the sense that we will deal with him.

The young Mandela had been given the tools to make a difference and learned some of the strategies needed to do so most effectively. Crucially, he also had the will to take up the gauntlet.

Challenge the Status Quo

'When people are determined,
they can overcome anything.'

NELSON MANDELA IN CONVERSATION
WITH MORGAN FREEMAN, 2006

M andela's heritage did not fill him with arrogance but it did supply him with a certain level of self-confidence that fed his instinctive refusal to bow to anyone without good reason. Undoubtedly, he was also imbued with a rebellious spirit from his earliest days. Nelson was not the name given him by his parents. Instead he was called Rolihlahla Mandela. Was there a certain glint in the eye that his parents quickly recognized? It seems possible, given that Rolihlahla may loosely be translated as 'trouble-maker'.

This inclination to challenge combined with a series of other factors in his youth to create a 'perfect storm'. His father's death propelled him early into the role of 'man of the household' so that as a pre-teen he already felt responsible for the fates of those around him. Meanwhile, his love of his homeland was unshakeable. Growing up in a traditional thatched hut and helping to raise livestock, phases of his childhood were idyllic. Rural South Africa came to represent a sort of earthly paradise for him – he would in later years speak wistfully of 'the veldt, the green open spaces, the simple beauty of nature, and the pure lines of the horizon'. Having been brought up within the Methodist Christian tradition, he would have been familiar with the idea of Eden. He was also aware that the native population had been and continued to be deprived of their Eden by the excesses of white rule.

By the time he was in his teens, Mandela – in common with teens everywhere – was ready and eager to kick against the world. His was no aimless rebellion, though. He was already fixing his focus on what would become his life's struggle. While in prison in the mid-1970s, he worked on a volume of autobiography that was never to be published. In it, he described how he felt his destiny even as a student: 'At college I had come to believe that as a graduate I would automatically be at the head, leading my people in all their efforts.'

A letter he wrote in 1976 from his cell on Robben Island to the then Commissioner of Prisons, Gen. Du Preez, offers further evidence of his indomitable spirit and his refusal to bow to others: 'I have never regarded any man as my superior, either in my life outside or inside prison.'

Like all the great rebels, he understood that his life's work would bring with it many setbacks to cope with. Indeed, dealing with the setbacks is part of the work. In 1998 he addressed a reception at the White House in Washington. By then his prison days were behind him and instead he was the celebrated President of the fully democratic 'Rainbow Nation'. But even then, the shadow of the youthful rebel was apparent as he highlighted the life-affirming nature of struggle: 'If our expectations – if our fondest prayers and dreams – are not realized, then we should all bear in mind that the greatest glory of living lies not in never falling, but in rising every time you fall.'

Embrace
Education

'Education is the most powerful weapon
which you can use to change the world.'

NELSON MANDELA AT THE LAUNCH OF
THE MINDSET NETWORK, 2003

I n a country where the illiteracy rate among the black population stood at around 90 per cent at the 1921 census, Mandela always valued the power of education to precipitate social progress. He was the first member of his family to attend school (according to Mandela: 'Mother could neither read nor write and had no means to send me to school'), going to a local Methodist-run institution from the age of seven with the financial assistance of his clan.

Indeed, it was on his first day at school that his teacher, a Miss Mdingane, announced that each pupil would be addressed by their new 'English name'. Mandela was given the name Nelson for reasons never made clear to him but presumably as a tribute to the great British admiral. It marked the beginning of Mandela's dual existence in which his classically African upbringing was balanced by a Western-style formal education.

Later, he would attend the (again Western-influenced) Clarkenbury Boarding Institute at Engcobo. With his rural background, he was considered something of a yokel there and, having enjoyed years of being treated with considerable deference at home, now found himself a peg or two down the prevailing social scale.

From Clarkenbury, he moved in 1937 to the Methodist Healdtown College in Fort Beaufort, in what is now the Eastern Cape. There, Mandela was educated so that he might become, in his own words, a 'black Englishman'. Though his formal education had a strong British bias – or perhaps *because* it did – the young Mandela was increasingly captivated by the history and culture of South Africa's indigenous populations.

He then won a place at the University of Fort Hare, which is to be found in the town of Alice. Established in 1916, it was the first South African university to offer Western-style higher education to non-whites and took the most promising students from throughout the continent. It was, therefore, considered the equivalent of an Oxbridge or Ivy League institution for the black population of the Southern Hemisphere. Mandela greatly enlarged his social horizons there, studying with young people from an array of backgrounds and with wildly differing outlooks. The university boasts alumni that include many famous names from Africa's post-colonial history including Kenneth Kaunda (first President of Zambia), Seretse Khama (Botswana's first President), Robert Mugabe (first President of Zimbabwe), Julius Nyerere (first President of Tanzania) and Desmond Tutu, who for a time served as its chaplain. Mandela would also forge one of the most important friendships of his life there when he met Oliver Tambo, his long-time ally in the ANC.

Although he left the University of Fort Hare without receiving his degree (he was expelled for his political activities but gained a BA through the University of South Africa in 1942), Mandela had all in all received a broad-based education that encompassed, *inter alia*, English, politics, anthropology and law. Nor was this the end of his formal education. He would go on to study Law at the University of Witwatersrand (again without graduating although he would complete his LLB with the University of South Africa in 1989) and also benefitted from the informal study groups that comprised the *ad hoc* 'University of Robben Island'.

Despite the prison authorities being inconsistent in allowing access to study materials, Mandela and many of his fellow inmates sought to further and share their knowledge. Many, for instance, took up correspondence courses and, in periods of more stringent control by the authorities, the prisoners continued to arrange both small and large discussion groups covering a wide range of disciplines. If particular books were banned, attempts were made to smuggle in suitable texts that were then copied word-for-word and distributed. In addition, those who had benefitted from formal education were encouraged to teach basic skills to those who had not.

Mandela remained acutely aware that the many achievements of his life would have been all but impossible were it not for the skills he developed as a boy and young man and which he continued to refine in later years. He commented: 'A good head and good heart are always a formidable combination. But when you add to that a literate tongue or pen, then you have something very special.' For him, education was the engine of personal development that allows, as he once put it, a peasant's daughter to aspire to be a doctor or the son of a mineworker to one day manage the mine. Education, in short, is the means to equality of opportunity.

In addition, he realized how vital education was in taking on an opponent. In his struggle to establish racial equality in South Africa, he knew the battle could never be won by force alone. His goals could only be achieved by winning hearts and minds too. As he would tell Richard Stengel – the one-time editor of *Time* magazine who assisted Mandela in the writing of *Long Walk to Freedom* and who ultimately became a trusted friend: 'When a man fights, even the enemies, you know, respect you, especially if you fight intelligently.'

He was also convinced that good education should strive not to engender hate but to teach its opposite, love. It is an ideal he expanded upon in *Long Walk to Freedom*:

The power of education extends beyond the development of skills we need for economic success. It can contribute to nation-building and reconciliation. Our previous system emphasized the physical and other differences of South Africans with devastating effects. We are steadily but surely introducing education that enables our children to exploit their similarities and common goals, while appreciating the strength in their diversity.

Healthy Body, Healthy Mind

'I have always believed exercise is a key not only
to physical health but to peace of mind.'

NELSON MANDELA, *LONG WALK TO FREEDOM*

M andela in his prime was a fine physical specimen: tall (measuring in at some 1.9 metres or 6 foot 3 inches) and well proportioned. A talented sportsman with skills embracing a number of disciplines, he understood the relationship (now well established by scientific research) between physical and mental wellbeing.

Consider, for instance, the advice he gave to his daughter, Maki, in a letter written while he was on Robben Island. 'Your physical condition,' he explained, 'especially the feeling of well-being after a good exercise, is closely related to your academic performance.' It was a sentiment echoed in a letter he wrote shortly before his release from prison to another of his children, Dumani. On that occasion, Mandela wrote of how taking part in 'sports like running, swimming and tennis will keep you healthy, strong and bright'.

He himself was a highly accomplished runner, a sport he no doubt loved in part for the opportunity it gave for quiet reflection on one's own and because of its demand for self-discipline. He told Maki that she should take the time to don a tracksuit and 'trot' around the running track on the basis that running not only gives you a sense of well-being but has the advantage of exercising all parts of the body.

EYE OF THE TIGER

However, of all the sports he practised, Mandela loved boxing above all others. This should come as little surprise, given its need not only for physical prowess but for self-discipline, strength of mind, bravery and a willingness to take on an opponent at close quarters.

The years around the time he came to national attention were a golden age for boxing. The heavyweight ranks were dominated by such legendary names as Floyd Patterson, Sonny Liston and Muhammad Ali. Each of these were black men who through dint of hard work and natural talent had achieved fame, riches and success, even while the society in which they operated was riven by racial prejudice. Boxing had, to an extent at least, provided them with a level playing field and offered an opportunity for progression and development that otherwise would almost certainly not have been available to them. This sense that all men are equal when the boxing gloves go on elevated the sport for Mandela, as he explained in *Long Walk to Freedom*: 'Boxing is egalitarian. In the ring, rank, age, colour and wealth are irrelevant. When you are circling your opponent, probing his strengths and weaknesses, you are not thinking about his colour or social status.'

Such was Mandela's deep-seated passion for the noble art that when he was asked to reflect on the various highs and lows of his life after his release from prison, he said he had but one regret – that he had never become heavyweight champion of the world. While he no doubt had his tongue lodged in his cheek at the time, it is likely that there was some truth behind the proclamation.

In certain lights, his career bears comparison with a boxing match. In one corner, the established but lumbering giant of the apartheid system. In the other, Mandela, the fleet-footed and defiant opponent, switching lightning-quick from defence to attack and back again. For round after round, Mandela takes extraordinary punishment from his bigger rival and at times all seems lost but he is blessed with a remarkable stamina and a seemingly granite jaw that allows him to resist one apparent knock-out blow after another. Then, in the final reckoning, his greater powers of endurance win out as his opponent, exhausted and devoid of ideas, collapses.

Such a comparison may at first seem frivolous but it is interesting to note that Mandela is by no means the only post-colonial black African leader to have boxed. Perhaps the most famous of the 'boxing presidents' was Uganda's Idi Amin, who was national light heavyweight champion throughout the 1950s and even challenged Tanzania's President, Julius Nyerere, to a boxing match when tensions became strained between their respective countries. Amin's legacy was one of mass murder and economic collapse and he does not warrant being bracketed with Mandela in terms of leadership, but we should perhaps not overlook the personal strength and tactical nous that both derived from their passion for ring craft.

Where boxing for Amin became another way to bully, for Mandela it was vital in helping him maintain control over his wilder instincts. When he might have wished to hit out at those who blocked his path, he realized instead that his purposes were better served by unleashing his pent up aggression in the gym. It also proved vital to maintain his emotional equilibrium during his years of incarceration. He eloquently explained its importance in his 1994 biography:

Many times in the old days I unleashed my anger and frustration on a punchbag rather than taking it out on a comrade or even a policeman. Exercise dissipates tension, and tension is the enemy of serenity. I found that I worked better and thought more clearly when

I was in good physical condition, and so training became one of the inflexible disciplines of my life. In prison, having an outlet for my frustrations was absolutely essential.

Learn the
Lessons of History

'For three centuries the whites have tried to tell
the black man that he has no history, civilization or
identity to be proud of; that only whites have a past,
a cultural heritage and a common awareness
of their mission in life.'

NELSON MANDELA, 'WHITHER THE BLACK
CONSCIOUSNESS MOVEMENT?', 1978

Allied to his passion for education, Mandela always displayed a strong instinctive feeling for history. Throughout his life, it was his heart-felt belief that, while the past is not a place in which we should seek to dwell, it is beholden upon us to seek to learn its lessons or pay a heavy price. He was convinced that an unwillingness to engage with the past – allied to the active suppression of history by those who wielded power – played a crucial part in keeping down the black population of South Africa. At the 2004 opening of the Nelson Mandela Centre of Memory, a Johannesburg-based organization that seeks to provide 'an integrated public information resource on his life and times', he commented: 'The history of our country is characterized by too much forgetting. A forgetting which served the powerful and dispossessed the weak.'

That apartheid was a crime against humanity is now a commonly accepted view and that it was able to sustain itself for as long as it did is a blight on human history. While the system relied upon oppression and physical violence to deal with those who opposed it, Mandela realized from his own academic studies that it was underpinned by a series of misconceptions often enshrined in the rhetoric of historical teaching that provided the intellectual justification among certain of the white elite to keep power for themselves. As Mandela argues in the quote above, the black population had to carry the fight against the apartheid system by reclaiming their own history and identity and, where necessary, wrestling it free from those who sought to deny it.

Throughout his long career of activism, he sought to communicate his own interpretations of history. When on trial for treason in the late 1950s, for instance, he took the opportunity to deconstruct the imperialist project. The great colonizing nations of Europe had long consoled themselves with the notion that imperialism was not only of material benefit to the colonizer but was a two-way street in which the colonized benefitted from the introduction of Western knowledge and 'civilization'. Mandela, though, was predictably having none of it. He did not hold back in attacking a system that he stated had 'gone all over the world subjugating people and exploiting them, bringing death and destruction to millions of people'.

In this same period he was a notably vociferous critic of the United States too, condemning its imperialist tendencies at a time when much of the world saw the US as the beacon of global freedom. While Washington did not operate an overt policy of invade-and-conquer, its ever-growing commercial and cultural reach coupled with a robust foreign policy created a sort of creeping hegemony that Mandela was quick to realize. 'The American brand of imperialism is imperialism all the same in spite of the modern clothing in which it is dressed and in spite of the sweet language spoken by its advocates and agents,' he wrote in 1958. While recognizing that twentieth-century Americans were not the same as the British and Dutch of the eighteenth and nineteenth centuries, he was determined that the lessons of the black South African experience should not be dismissed.

Nor was this the posturing of a young firebrand. Mandela maintained his distrust of colonialism into old age. Take the following passage, which he wrote in 1998 in what was intended to be a follow-up volume of autobiography to *Long Walk to Freedom* (but which in the event was never published):

The plundering of indigenous land, exploitation of its mineral wealth and other raw materials, confinement of its people to specific areas, and the restriction of their movement have, with notable exceptions, been the cornerstones of colonialism throughout the land.

Crucially, Mandela strove to incorporate the lessons of history into his world view without binding himself to dogma. He was a product of Africa and, understandably, expressed suspicion of the West for its historical role on that continent. However, he was always outward looking and has understood that there is intellectual capital to be mined from all cultures. In defence of himself during the Rivonia Trial in 1964 (see page 98), he laid out how he intended to go about reaping the benefits:

> I have been influenced in my thinking by both West and East. All this has led me to feel that in my search for a political formula, I should be absolutely impartial and objective. I should tie myself to no particular system of society other than of socialism. I must leave myself free to borrow the best from the West and from the East.

This receptiveness to the lessons offered up by history was undoubtedly a key factor in his development as a history-maker in his own right.

How to Eat and Drink like Nelson

'Can we drink whisky?'

NELSON MANDELA IN
MANDELA: THE LIVING LEGEND, 2003

When looking at great lives, the role of food and drink has not necessarily always been given the consideration it deserves. Yet in the case of Mandela, it is highly instructive. Not only does it provide us with an insight into his personal tastes and cultural influences, but it can also be seen as a window through which we can trace some of the broader trajectories of his life.

Here was someone born into the upper echelons of a traditional African tribal system, a fact reflected in his diet. By the time he was a young adult, Mandela cut a fine and healthy figure and the tastes developed in his youth would remain with him into old age. The joyful memory of roasting corn beneath a vast night sky, for instance, is one that never left him.

Then came the almost-three decades that he spent in jail, when his relationship with food changed from one of active enjoyment to a certain degree of passivity. Consumption was limited to what the prison authorities provided, with even the decision as to when to eat taken away from the prisoner. This was also a period when he, along with other inmates, used hunger strikes as a way of protesting against mistreatment and poor conditions. In this way, food, or at least its non-consumption, became a medium through which Mandela could continue to carry his fight to the oppressor. Rendered largely powerless by incarceration, starving oneself perversely became a way of wielding some control.

A letter he wrote from Robben Island to his wife, Winnie, in 1970 gives a clue as to how thoughts of food (or more specifically, its absence) could play on the mind. 'I long for *amasi*,' he wrote, 'the food for which I loved to sharpen my teeth and to stretch out my tummy, the one I really enjoyed.' *Amasi* is a thick, fermented milk drink, a little like plain yoghurt and noted for its health benefits. In fact, such was Mandela's love for it that in *Long Walk to Freedom* he related how he once almost gave away his hiding place when he was living *incommunicado*. He had left some *amasi* on the window sill of an apartment in which he was secreted in a white area of town. He then overheard two local workers comment on how unusual it was to see *amasi* in such a neighbourhood, as it was rarely drunk by the non-black population.

Mandela revealed that his favourite foods in prison included fish cakes, poached eggs and biryani (a spiced rice dish of Southeast Asian origin). This latter food was one that held particular resonance as it reminded him of his time living underground, when biryanis were a staple given to him by allies in the Indian Congress.

Eventually he was put on to a cholesterol-free diet but on one occasion found himself in the prison hospital suffering from tuberculosis. He was brought a hearty plate of bacon and eggs before a doctor stepped in to advise him that he should not eat it. Mandela, though, was having none of the doctor's advice. 'Today I am prepared to die,' he told him. 'I am going to eat it.' Out of prison, meanwhile, he was an avowed coffee drinker but in prison he drank tea and was especially fond of rooibos (which translates as 'red bush'), made from a shrub native to South Africa.

Life post-release must have come as quite a shock to Mandela's taste buds and belly. Having spent so long faced with a greatly restricted diet, he now found himself travelling the world, eating at high-end establishments and attending countless banquets in his honour. Yet it was the food of his childhood that he really desired. As his personal chef since the early 1990s, Xoliswa Ndoyiya, revealed, he 'preferred the traditional fare'.

A noted early-riser, he began his day with a simple breakfast typically consisting of plain porridge and fresh fruit, washed down with milk. *Amasi* remained a favourite too, as did another fermented drink, *amarhewu*, which is made from corn-meal. Later in the day, he was keen on peppery foods and was on record as a fan of freshly slaughtered lamb or mutton. Other traditional foods sure to meet with approval included *umsila wenkomo* (a sort of oxtail stew) and *dombolo* (dumplings).

Such is the interest in Mandela's dining habits that the Mandela Centre of Memory has even published a volume of his favourite recipes as compiled by Xoliswa Ndoyiya, entitled *Ukutya Kwasekhaya: Tastes from Nelson*

Mandela's Kitchen. Through the food he loved, we can better understand how his background and culture influenced the man that the world embraced.

Find Your Cause

'Men, I think, are not capable of doing nothing, of saying nothing, of not reacting to injustice, of not protesting against oppression, of not striving for the good society and the good life in the ways they see it.'

NELSON MANDELA, 1962

B y the time he was a student, Mandela had become politically active. As we have seen, he was expelled from Fort Hare University in 1940 after involvement in protests rooted in the alleged mistreatment of a canteen worker and a stand-off over university electoral procedures. It was early evidence that Mandela could not stand by when he perceived injustice.

After his expulsion, he was faced with the prospect of a marriage arranged by his disappointed guardian, Jongintaba. Mandela's response was to flee to Johannesburg in the company of Jongintaba's own son, Justice. Once in the big city, the next stage of Mandela's political awakening occurred.

Until then, his social status and relative wealth had insulated him from many of the harsher realities of his society. In Johannesburg, though, the scales fell away from his eyes. Although apartheid was not yet the government's official policy, it was obvious just how weighted against the black population life was. Mandela talked of the 'thousand indignities' he witnessed every day. He was also exposed to a new level of political activism, such as the 1943 Alexandra bus boycott, which was organized by a well-known activist called Gaur Radebe to protest against the cost of travel, quality of service and so on. This was a step on from the student protests with which Mandela was already familiar.

Coinciding with his move to Johannesburg was the revitalization of the African National Congress (ANC) under the leadership of Alfred Xuma. The ANC had been founded in 1912 and had made its mark as a petitioning organization but became far more dynamic in the 1940s. In 1944 an offshoot Youth League (ANCYL) was founded and Mandela was appointed as its secretary, with responsibility for boosting membership. He also held a place on the ANC executive for the Transvaal.

1948 saw the victory of the Afrikaner National Party at a general election, having campaigned on the apartheid ticket. Two years later Mandela became president of the ANCYL and oversaw a programme of mass action reminiscent of those led by Gandhi in pre-independence India. The aim was simple: to bring an end to discrimination on the basis of race. As Mandela would put it during the Rivonia trial: 'We believe that South Africa belongs to all the people who live in it, and not to one group, be it black or white.'

This is the key tenet of Mandela's career. Not for him the blurriness of, say, the Black Panthers so prominent in the US civil rights movement whose call for an end to racism at times became immersed in anti-white rhetoric. Mandela's philosophy, by contrast, was always about equality for all, as he explained during legal proceedings in 1962: 'I want at once to make it clear that I am no racialist, and I detest racialism, because I regard it as a barbaric thing, whether it comes from a black man or from a white man.'

It was a theme he was proud to return to a full forty-three years later in Johannesburg at a commemoration of the lives of two prominent activists, Yusuf Cachalia of the South African Indian Congress and the civil rights lawyer, Bram Fischer. Mandela told the gathering:

I hope that our movement will always hold that commitment to non-racialism dear in its thoughts, policies and actions. It is that commitment, even in circumstances where we could have been pardoned for deviating from it, that amongst other things earned us the respect of the world.

APARTHEID

According to the *Concise Oxford Dictionary*, apartheid is 'a policy or system of segregation or discrimination on grounds of race'. In practice, it was among the most pernicious power frameworks put into operation anywhere during the twentieth century.

Apartheid was introduced by the National Party, which held power from 1948 until 1994, initially under the leadership of D. F. Malan. The party had been founded in 1915 as the voice of the Afrikaner minority and came into government intent on promoting the interests of that minority to the detriment of the majority. Every aspect of normal life was impacted. Marriage between whites and non-whites was outlawed, while many jobs were reserved for whites only. Blacks were also faced with a far lower quality of education, health and public service provision.

In 1950 came the Registration Act, which classified every individual as either White, Black, Coloured (i.e. those of mixed race) or Indian. It was a piece of legislation loaded with value judgements; to be designated 'white', for instance, not only was parentage considered but also 'habits, education, and speech and deportment and demeanour'. Blacks were required to carry what were known as pass books, containing a photo of the holder along with a wealth of personal information, including name, address, tax code, fingerprints and employment history. Employers could even enter an assessment of an individual into the pass book.

The pass book could trace its origins back to 1797, when Earl Macartney introduced a comparable system in his time as Governor of the Cape Colony. A series of subsequent Pass Laws were implemented to general unpopularity, prompting notable resistance campaigns in 1906, 1919 and in the 1930s. Under the National Party from 1948, the Pass Laws were implemented with renewed vigour. Blacks were required to carry their documentation when travelling outside their designated areas and failure to produce a valid pass could result in arrest and imprisonment. Women were included in the system from the 1950s and the pass book requirement was only overturned in 1986.

The 1960s and 1970s was the period of 'Grand Apartheid'. A series of constitutional reforms were passed by parliament so that by the 1970s only whites had the right to vote in national elections. In search of racial homogenization, white-only areas were expanded and the black population became increasingly marginalized in poor and ill-served townships of their own. Then the creation of ten self-governing 'black homelands' saw millions deprived of their citizenship.

The authorities stamped down hard on protest of any sort – both violent and non-violent. People could be detained for months at a stretch without recourse to due process and thousands died while in custody. It was for them, and millions more who were downtrodden in this state-run system of oppression, that Mandela waged his fight for justice.

Focus on Personal Development

'It is what we make out of what we have, not what we are given, that separates one person from another.'

NELSON MANDELA, *LONG WALK TO FREEDOM*

Having identified the cause that would dominate his life, Mandela did not wildly rail against his enemies but took time to develop himself so that he might better take up the struggle. At the heart of his search for personal development was an unyielding belief that in a battle between right and wrong there can only be one winner. As he wrote in a letter from his prison cell in 1976: 'The simple lesson of all religions, of all philosophies and of life itself is that, although evil may be on the rampage temporarily, the good must win the laurels in the end.'

Mandela's experiences in 1940s Johannesburg would prove crucial to his personal growth. Arriving in the city with very little, he first took a job as a night watchman at a mining compound – a job he lost after a disgruntled Jongintaba intervened. However, Mandela eventually persuaded the regent that he be allowed to stay in the city so that he could continue his studies. He moved to the poor Alexandra neighbourhood, where he mixed with people from a wide variety of backgrounds and, critically, was introduced to Walter Sisulu. As Mandela would later say: 'Alexandra occupies a treasured place in my heart. It was the first place I lived away from home.'

Mandela took a job as a clerk with a legal firm after an introduction from Sisulu and he would subsequently enrol for a law degree at the University of Witwatersrand, where his social horizons were further broadened as he met a student body straddling all races and political inclinations. Away from the academic world, he was to be found socializing in the Sophiatown neighbourhood, which at the time was a multicultural hub, vibrant, cool and fizzing with ideas. It may be seen as South Africa's very own version of 1920s and '30s Harlem. As Mandela sought to fit in here, the experience undoubtedly made him more streetwise, an attribute that would serve him well throughout his life.

As the 1940s proceeded he became ever more involved with the ANC. By the end of the decade he had failed to secure his law degree but had taken the necessary exams so that he could practice professionally. In 1952 he and Oliver Tambo, his old friend from the Fort Hare days, set up the country's first black-owned legal firm. Mandela was a natural and persuasive performer in front of judges and juries and it has been said that his greatest oratory took place within the theatre of the courtroom.

By his mid-thirties, Mandela had established himself as a prominent figure within Johannesburg's – and, increasingly, South Africa's – political and legal spheres. He was also learning to temper his natural firebrand tendencies. In later life he would look back on his younger self as very radical, prone to employing high-flown language and keen to fight everybody in sight.

The famous 'No Easy Walk to Freedom' speech he made to the ANC Transvaal Congress in 1953 gives a hint of the fiery temperament that can be hard to reconcile with the much gentler public image he adopted in his later years: 'The racial policies of the Government have pricked the conscience of all men of good will and have aroused their deepest indignation. The feelings of the oppressed people have never been more bitter.'

Somewhat counter-intuitively, it was his years in prison that knocked off some of his rough edges. When we might have expected him to become more radical and, indeed, angrier, he in fact became more self-composed though his commitment to his cause never wavered. His prison experience was undoubtedly a brutal one that left its scars but it is emblematic of Mandela's remarkable fortitude that he responded to those long years of incarceration by developing ever more rational approaches and embracing compromise in the hope of achieving his ultimate goals. In his 1976 'National Liberation' essay he wrote:

My current circumstances give me advantages my compatriots outside jail rarely have. Here the past literally rushes to memory and there is plenty of time for reflection. One is able to stand back and look at the entire movement from a distance, and the bitter lessons of prison life force one to go all out to win cooperation of all fellow prisoners, to learn how to see problems from the point of view of others as well, and to work smoothly with other schools of thought in the movement.

In 1970 he had written a letter to Winnie in which he looked back on his former self, whose ideas he considered to be derivative. Robben Island had made him, he wrote, more reflective, open to others and self-disciplined. He was also aware that all this could manifest itself in a self-containment that to others might seem like aloofness – a conclusion that highlights his ability to recognize his own faults. Overall, though, the period of enforced self-reflection caused him to re-evaluate his priorities, as he set out in another letter written to Winnie, this one in 1975:

> In judging our progress as individuals we tend to focus on external factors such as one's social position, influence and popularity, wealth and standard of education… but internal factors may be even more crucial in assessing one's development as a human being: honesty, sincerity, simplicity, humility, purity, generosity, absence of vanity, readiness to serve your fellow men – qualities within the reach of every soul – are the foundations of one's spiritual life…

These conclusions were instrumental in the formulation of his guiding philosophy of ethical leadership.

Having had his freedoms taken from him, he became increasingly aware of the need to seize opportunities as they presented themselves and to approach problems with a fundamental sense of optimism. He was evermore convinced that to take advantage of opportunity, one must plan all the details of one's life so that we 'allow the intervention of fate only on our own terms'.

In 2002, at the ninetieth birthday celebrations of his friend Walter Sisulu, Mandela reflected on what makes a worthwhile life. It was, perhaps, the perfect summation of his many decades of personal development: 'What counts in life is not the mere fact that we have lived. It is what difference we have made to the lives of others that will determine the significance of the life we lead.'

THE FREEDOM CHARTER

The Freedom Charter was adopted by the ANC and its Congress Alliance partners in 1955. It served as a statement of core principles, many of which would be incorporated into South Africa's post-apartheid constitution. It also serves as a good indicator of Mandela's personal position as established by the 1950s. The beginning of the Charter reads:

We, the People of South Africa, declare for all our country and the world to know:
⊙ that South Africa belongs to all who live in it, black and white, and that no government can

justly claim authority unless it is based on the will of all the people;

- that our people have been robbed of their birthright to land, liberty and peace by a form of government founded on injustice and inequality;
- that our country will never be prosperous or free until all our people live in brotherhood, enjoying equal rights and opportunities;
- that only a democratic state, based on the will of all the people, can secure to all their birthright without distinction of colour, race, sex or belief;
- And therefore, we, the people of South Africa, black and white together equals, countrymen and brothers adopt this Freedom Charter;
- And we pledge ourselves to strive together, sparing neither strength nor courage, until the democratic changes here set out have been won.

Progress Starts
with the Self

'A new world will be won not by those who stand
at a distance with their arms folded, but by those
who are in the arena, whose garments are torn by
storms and whose bodies are maimed in the
course of the contest.'

NELSON MANDELA, 1969

Among Mandela's many attributes, his sense of personal responsibility and his willingness to be self-critical are especially marked. Here is a man who refused to shy away from difficult situations and who strove to be the best that he can be in the service of others. His insatiable desire to improve the lot of his fellow man provided him with the resources he needed to endure extraordinary hardships. His life, in certain lights at least, is almost a model of selflessness and his willingness to 'step up to the mark' was neatly summed up in a speech he gave at the Nelson Mandela Foundation in 2004: 'There can be no greater gift than that of giving one's time and energy to help others without expecting anything in return.'

He repeatedly encouraged his colleagues and supporters to look inwards in pursuit of their collective goals. Speaking at a banquet in Cape Town in 2002, for instance, he urged the assembled gathering to be 'masters of our own fate'. 'No longer shall we seek,' he told them, 'to place blame for our condition elsewhere or to look to others to take responsibility for our development.'

His sentiments echoed those he had delivered two

years earlier in London, UK, at the launch of the Final
Report of the World Commission on Dams:

> It has been easy to blame all of our troubles on a
> faceless system: the Crown; the church; hierarchy;
> globalisation; multinational corporations; the Apartheid
> state. It is not a hard task to place blame. But we
> must look within ourselves, become responsible and
> provide fresh solutions if we ever want to do more
> than complain, or make excuses.

Nor were these ideas that he had developed from the
position of power he then commanded. In 1976, while
imprisoned on Robben Island, he wrote an essay entitled
'Clear the obstacles and confront the enemy'. In it, he
exhorted: 'We should concentrate more on constructive
self-criticism and on frankly and publicly acknowledging
our own mistakes to our own people. Far from being a
sign of weakness, it is a measure of one's strength and
confidence, which will pay dividends in the end.'

He did acknowledge that the process of critical
self-analysis followed by making necessary changes to
one's life can be hard. In a speech in 2000, for instance,
he spoke of how, in order to be an effective agent for
peace, an individual must look to change his community
and the wider world. However, he pointed out, before
that could be achieved we face the far tougher task of
changing ourselves.

If we are unprepared to make the necessary changes

to ourselves, the chances of achieving broader aims are greatly limited. In effect, the person who demands social change but refuses to start closer to home may be accused of being 'all talk and no action' – a position that was anathema to Mandela. As he pointed out in his 1978 'Whither the Black Consciousness Movement?' essay: 'Preparing a master plan and applying it are two different things.'

There were periods of Mandela's life when he had been so stripped of power and authority that the ability to control his own self and state of mind was the only control he could exert. Thus introspection, self-criticism and responsive change – while sometimes painful in their own right – were an integral part of Mandela's survival mechanism. While he could change himself for the better, he retained hope and while he retained that, he had not succumbed to his enemy. In a letter he sent to Winnie from Robben Island in 1969 he would talk of hope as a powerful weapon and a power of which no one can deprive you. He touched upon the idea again in *Long Walk to Freedom*: 'There were many dark moments when my faith in humanity was sorely tested, but I would not and could not give myself up to despair. That way lay defeat and death.'

Elsewhere in his autobiography he related how he once had a run-in with Lieutenant Prins, the head of the prison on Robben Island. Mandela was in dispute with him after a visit from Winnie was blocked and he took exception to what he considered was a slur Prins had made against his wife. Though he restrained himself from making a physical attack, Mandela unleashed a volley of abuse that he quickly regretted. 'He had caused me to violate my self-control,' he wrote, 'and I consider that a defeat at the hands of my opponent.' As he had noted in 1971: 'It has been said a thousand and one times that what matters is not so much what happens to a person than the way such person takes it.'

For Mandela, the interests of the many and the actions of the individual were bound together. We cannot begin to set about achieving a grand goal (e.g. overturning the apartheid system) without first taking responsibility for our own actions. Equally, while we have the capability to exert control over ourselves, we have the hope to achieve much greater things.

There is also a pragmatic advantage to this: displays of self-control and self-change win you admirers. What is great leadership, after all, if not the quality of taking responsibility for your actions and directing them towards a wider good. In a letter to his daughter in 1969, Mandela spoke of how human beings like to be associated with hard-working, disciplined and successful people and that cultivating these qualities secures you friends and allies. Once out of prison, he continued to put emphasis on pursuing personally high standards. He told the crowd who had gathered at his 'Welcome Home' rally in Soweto in 1990: 'I call in the strongest possible way for us to act with the dignity and discipline that our just struggle for freedom deserves.'

And in 2004 he sent a message to the Global Convention on Peace and Nonviolence, which was meeting at the time in New Delhi. It serves as a rousing injunction to embrace change, starting with ourselves:

Human beings will always be able to find arguments for confrontation and no compromise. We humans are, however, the beings capable of reason, compassion and change. May this be the century of compassion, peace and non-violence: here in this region where you meet, in all the conflict-ridden parts of the world, and on our planet universally.

Reset the Moral Compass: The Path From Civil Disobedience to Armed Struggle

'I can only say that I felt morally
obliged to do what I did.'

NELSON MANDELA'S RIVONIA
TRIAL STATEMENT, 1964

Until his death, Mandela was the pre-eminent 'grand old statesman', respected and courted by virtually every other political leader alive. It is therefore easy to forget that right up until his release from prison, there were those who considered him a dangerous terrorist. For instance, the British Prime Minister, Margaret Thatcher, said in 1987 (just three years before Mandela's release from prison to a hero's reception): 'The ANC is a typical terrorist organization ... Anyone who thinks it is going to run the government in South Africa is living in cloud-cuckoo land.'

Any analysis of Mandela's life must, though, attempt to trace his transition from exponent of non-violent protest to the taking up of arms. Tracking the progression is not simple and made even more complex by the truth of the old maxim that one man's freedom fighter is another man's terrorist, However, it is evident that the decision to use violence against the apartheid system was not one rushed into or taken in anger. It was instead the result of a long and painful process of introspection that left Mandela and his colleagues convinced that their demands would never be met if they maintained their campaigns of non-violent protest only. As Mandela would argue at the funeral of Oliver Tambo in 1993:

> There are many who did not understand that to heal we had to lance the boil. There are many who still do not understand that the obedient silence of the enslaved is not the reward of peace which is our due. There are some who cannot comprehend that the right to rebellion against tyranny is the very guarantee of the permanence of freedom.

The ANC was founded in 1912 in response to the eroding of black rights perpetrated by the national government. After a brief burst of energy directed against, for instance, land reforms and the Pass Laws, there followed a prolonged period of ineffectiveness that spanned from the mid-1920s until the 1940s. Then Alfred Xuma reformed it into the mass movement with which we associate the young Mandela.

In terms of making a mark, the ANC's 1952 Defiance Campaign was of enormous importance and was arguably the peak of the era of non-violent protest in South Africa. The idea was for a mass mobilization, with citizens encouraged to challenge what the ANC had identified as six unjust laws. By breaking these laws and being sent to prison, the theory went, activists would draw national and international attention to their grievances. In short, they hoped to show up the government as unjust, reactionary and intransigent. In addition, the

ANC hoped that as people challenged injustice and lived to tell the tale, some of the fear factor associated with prison, the police, the army and the institutions of state might be removed. It was thought that fear of these institutions had hitherto had a paralysing effect on many who might otherwise have challenged apartheid.

It is estimated that some 8,500 people were imprisoned as a result of the campaign. The government responded with a predictably heavy hand and Mandela himself was arrested in July that year for his flouting of the Suppression of Communism Act. The ANC hierarchy considered the campaign a great success. Mandela himself would say: '… the white man had felt the power of my punches and I could walk upright like a man, and look everyone in the eye with the dignity that comes from not having succumbed to oppression and fear.' The Defiance Campaign marked his coming of age as a freedom fighter.

Yet while the campaign doubtlessly had a positive effect on those who took part in it, it achieved very little in precipitating a change in approach from the government. In fact, quite the reverse as the National Party sought to crush those who opposed it and implemented unpopular legislation like the Pass Laws with a new energy. There were more personalized attacks from the Establishment too. For instance, in 1954 the Law Society of Transvaal attempted to have Mandela struck off. Had they been successful, his professional career would have been at an end.

In 1956 over 150 people related to the Defiance Campaign and the Congress of the People (a grouping of various anti-apartheid groups that met in 1955 and from which the Freedom Charter emerged) were arrested and charged with treason. Albert Lutuli, who would later serve as ANC President, recalled the pre-dawn raids 'deliberately calculated to strike terror into hesitant minds and impress upon the entire nation the determination of the governing clique to stifle all opposition'. The resulting so-called Treason Trial ran for an energy-sapping five years before all the accused were acquitted in 1961. By that time, Mandela and Tambo's legal firm had been run into the ground under the strain of the proceedings and Tambo himself had been forced into exile.

Mandela had for several years suspected a change of tactics would be needed. In the 1950s he helped develop a cell-structure for the ANC, which it was hoped would allow it to continue working effectively in the event of it being banned. 1961 was a crucial year in the transition from non-violence to militancy. South Africa was by then also reeling from the events that had occurred at Sharpeville the previous year (see page 60). Mandela himself was under no illusion that they faced anything other than a 'white minority regime bent on retaining power at any cost'. The government's over-reaction to a stay-at-home protest (in effect, a general strike) on 31 May 1961, to mark the birth of the republic of South Africa, effectively brought to an end the era of purely peaceful protests. The authorities responded with a massive show of force, which included ordering a general mobilization, overseeing mass arrests of black Africans and giving arms to white communities. Faced with such provocation, Mandela sensed the futility of total reliance on non-violent tactics. He was also picking up on the increasing discontent among the ANC's grassroots support who were shocked at the savage tactics that the government had used against unarmed and defenceless people.

In July 1961 Mandela was present at the meeting that birthed the ANC's armed wing, Umkhonto we Sizwe ('Spear of the Nation'; abbreviated to MK). It was established with the aim of taking 'the struggle to the heart of white power'. Mandela was appointed its Commander-in-Chief and was clear in his mind that this was not to be a terrorist organization launching attacks on innocent civilians. Instead, it would focus on targeted sabotage. The aim, as he would explain to Richard Stengel many years later, was to conduct 'dignified guerrilla warfare' that was guided by principles and searched out the symbols of oppression.

The MK's manifesto was delivered in December 1961 and stated: 'The time comes in the life of any nation where there remain only two choices: submit or fight. That time has now come in South Africa.' It launched its first wave of attacks on 16 December 1961, exploding bombs in assorted government buildings and electricity substations across three cities. Mandela quoted a traditional proverb: 'Sebatana ha se bokwe ka diatla' ('The attacks of the wild beast cannot be averted with only bare hands').

Early in 1962 Mandela made a speech to the Conference of the Pan-African Freedom Movement of East and Central Africa outlining why focussed sabotage had become a vital *modus operandi*:

> But in a country where freedom fighters frequently pay with their very lives and at a time when the most elaborate military preparations are being made to crush the people's struggles, planned acts of sabotage against government installations introduce a new phase in the political situation and are a demonstration of the people's unshakeable determination to win freedom whatever the cost may be.

At his trial in 1962 for inciting strikes the previous year and for leaving the country without permission, Mandela seized the opportunity to justify his actions: 'I was made, by the law, a criminal, not because of what I had done, but because of what I stood for, because of what I thought, because of my conscience.' In circumstances where he and his fellow defendants could face jail and disruption to all aspects of their lives for undertaking peaceful forms of protest, it was little wonder that Mandela and his cohorts had lost patience with non-violence as their principle course of action.

As the trial progressed, he made a number of statements that provide us with a snapshot of his growing frustration with the failure of the non-violent approach:

Throughout its fifty years of existence the African National Congress, for instance, has done everything possible to bring its demands to the attention of successive South African governments. It has sought at all times peaceful solutions for all the country's ills and problems... In the face of the complete failure of the government to heed, to consider, or even to respond to our seriously proposed objections and our solutions to the forthcoming republic, what were we to do? Were we to allow the law which states that you shall not commit an offence by way of protest, to take its course and thus betray our conscience and our belief? Were we to uphold our conscience and our beliefs to strive for what we believe is right, not just for us, but for all the people who live in this country, both the present generation and for generations to come, and thus transgress against the law?...The government behaved in a way no civilized government should dare behave when faced with a peaceful, disciplined, sensible, and democratic expression of the views of its own population. It ordered the mobilization of its armed forces to attempt to cow and terrorise our peaceful protest.

He concluded with an ominous warning:

Government violence can only do one thing and that is to bring counter-violence. If there is no dawning of sanity on the part of the government, the dispute between the government and my people will finish up being settled in violence and by force.

By then, of course, Mandela had read extensively on military strategy and had travelled widely to mine the experience of those more experienced in armed freedom-fighting. As he put it himself, he made 'a study of the art of war and revolution'. Though now wedded to pursuing armed struggle, he nonetheless regarded it as the course of last resort following the comprehensive failure of peaceful protest.

Just as he had used his 1962 trial as a soapbox from which to speak to the wider world, he did so again during the Rivonia trial in 1964 (see page 98). Confronted with decisive evidence that he had planned acts of violence, he set out his reasons for doing so:

I do not, however, deny that I planned sabotage. I did not plan it in a spirit of recklessness, nor because I have any love of violence. I planned it as a result of a calm and sober assessment of the political situation that had arisen after many years of tyranny, exploitation, and oppression of my people by the Whites.

Even the judge was forced to concede that he believed the organization had taken care not to injure civilians.

Mandela also declared that the ANC had spent many years doing all it could to avoid civil war but its leaders realized that the actions of the MK made civil war a distinct possibility. However, he argued that the armed struggle was rooted not in aggression but was a defensive action against the violence imposed by the apartheid system. It was a case he made elegantly to the then Prime Minister, P. W. Botha, in a note sent in mid-1989 from Victor Verster Prison, where he was held for the final three years of his imprisonment:

> The position of the ANC on the question of violence is very simple. The organization has no vested interest in violence. It abhors any action which may cause loss of life, destruction of property and misery to the people. It has worked long and patiently for a South Africa of common values and for an undivided and peaceful non-racial state. But we consider the armed struggle a legitimate form of self-defence against a morally repugnant system of government which will not allow even peaceful form of protest.

In his post-release life, Mandela continued to ponder the question of non-violence against violence. He repeatedly emphasized that he was made an outlaw by the refusal of the government to allow the black majority the right to live the life to which they were entitled. He also argued that the ANC always stuck to its basic position of non-violence, only departing from it when circumstances demanded. He explained in *Long Walk to Freedom* that he regarded non-violence not as a moral principle but as a strategy and 'there is no moral goodness in using an ineffective weapon'.

So why, then, the turn towards armed struggle? Because, when push came to shove, there was no realistic alternative against an unbending oppressor. As Mandela put it in a speech in mitigation after his 1962 conviction for inciting strikes: 'To men, freedom in their own land is the pinnacle of their ambitions, from which nothing can turn men of conviction aside.'

THE SHARPEVILLE MASSACRE

In bringing international attention to the injustices of the apartheid system, there was arguably no single more important event than the slaughter that occurred in the township of Sharpeville, located between the cities of Vanderbijlpark and Vereeniging in what was then the Transvaal (and which is now part of Gauteng province).

As we have already seen, under the apartheid regime blacks were subject to the hugely unpopular Pass Laws that forced them to carry identification papers that served as an internal passport. The law stated that anyone found in a public place without their book could be arrested and detained for up to thirty days. So it was that

1960 had been designated by the ANC as the Year of the Pass and a campaign of nationwide popular protest and mass action was planned.

On 21 March 1960, a crowd estimated at somewhere between 5,000 and 10,000 gathered around the township's municipal offices and police station. While the protest was focussed on the Pass Laws, demonstrators wanted to draw attention to several other grievances, including high rents, low wages, the lack of trade union recognition and the 'colour bar' prohibiting blacks from holding certain kinds of jobs. All in all, the atmosphere was tense.

As the day progressed, the police grew increasingly nervous. There were perhaps twenty officers in attendance initially but they soon called for reinforcements until there were up to 300 policemen in the vicinity. The crowd was growing restive and some reports claimed that stones and rocks were thrown, though this is contentious. Regardless of the precise circumstances, it is beyond dispute that the police opened fire on the throng without warning, shooting randomly. Whether or not a specific order was given to fire continues to be debated.

Pandemonium ensued and an eye-witness described seeing civilians fleeing 'like rabbits'. By the time the shooting was over, some sixty-nine people were dead, including eight women and ten children. A further 180 lay injured, fifty of them women or children. Many had been shot in the back.

The local Police Commander, a certain D. H. Pienaar, subsequently gave his take on events. The few sentences he spoke encapsulated for many the fundamental disregard for the basic human rights of non-whites that was inherent in the apartheid system. 'It started when hordes of natives surrounded the police station,' he said. 'If they do these things, they must learn their lessons the hard way.'

The events of that day set in motion South Africa's increasing international isolation. The United Nations Security Council and governments worldwide spoke out to condemn the action of the police in Sharpeville as well as the apartheid policies that had created the climate in which such an atrocity could occur. The National Party government declared a state of emergency and just a week later, on 8 April 1960, passed the Unlawful Organizations Act that allowed for bans against the ANC and the Pan African Congress.

The world was now watching.

Inspire by Example

'If there is any significant role that I played, it was
that of being a vessel through which the struggle was
presented to the nation and the world. The struggle
had to have a symbol for it to be effective. The great
men and women of the struggle chose that I be the
symbol. If this was a good thing, praise must go to
those who made the choice.'

NELSON MANDELA IN INTERVIEW WITH
OPRAH WINFREY, 2000

M andela was born into a culture of tribal leadership and naturally took to leadership himself. He understood that leadership is more art than science and that it must evolve over time. From youthful, impassioned activist to great statesman in old age, his life provides a unique case study of inspirational leadership. So what lessons might we learn?

- ⊙ Impart your vision. In one of his personal notebooks from 1993, Mandela set out what he believed were the leader's chief tasks. The first, he concluded, is for the leader to create a vision and the second to assemble a team who will help him implement it. The second aspect will only succeed if the leader has properly communicated the vision and given the followers reason to buy into it.
- ⊙ Be consistent. He was always acutely aware of the need for constancy in his conduct – a significant challenge given the perpetually changing demands placed upon him. Again, it was a theme he investigated in his personal notebooks, in

which he concluded that leaders fall into one of two categories: those who are inconsistent and unpredictable, agreeing on a major issue one day and repudiating it the following day, and those who show consistency and 'have a sense of honour, a vision'.

▶ Be remarkable and unremarkable. Mandela was blessed with an innate ability to seem at once both exceptional and everyman-ish. Those who met him in person were made to feel, even if only briefly, as if they were the only person in the world that mattered. He always had the gift of self-effacement too, an attribute that both charms and disarms. Consider this statement from his 1962 trial: 'I sometimes believe that through me Creation intended to give the world the example of a mediocre man in the proper sense of the term.'

▶ Back yourself. This was never more evident than when Mandela undertook secret talks with the government, risking the wrath of his ANC colleagues for what he was sure was the greater good. He told Richard Stengel in 2003: 'It is absolutely necessary at times for the leader to take an independent action without consulting anybody and to present what he has done to the organization.'

▶ Maintain your dignity. If anyone could have been forgiven for a bit of triumphalist rabble-rousing, it was Mandela when he was released after twenty-seven years in jail. Instead he emerged the model of integrity. He remained dignified, open and apparently unencumbered by bitterness over the months and years of tricky political negotiations that followed.

▶ Offer hope. Mandela's life was dogged by difficulties and suffering yet he always maintained belief that he would succeed in his goals. It is an attitude encapsulated in a speech he made in 1993 on the announcement of the polling date for democratic elections: 'We can build a society grounded on friendship and our common humanity – a society founded on tolerance. That is the only road open to us. It is a road to a glorious future in this beautiful country of ours. Let us join hands and march into the future.'

▶ Mark the big moments. Mandela may not have been the greatest of orators but he nonetheless tended to hit upon the right words at the right time. Never more so than at his presidential inauguration in 1994: 'Never, never and never again shall it be that this beautiful land will again experience the oppression of one by another… Let freedom reign.'

▶ Encourage others to be the best versions of them-selves. A task Mandela achieved with extraordinary success, especially given the brutalization to which he himself was exposed over his lifetime. The following words he delivered in early 1999 on receiving the Deutscher Medienpreis give a taste of his ability to inspire: 'If the experience of South Africa means anything to the world at large, we hope that it is in having demonstrated that where people of goodwill get together and transcend their differences for the common good, peaceful and just solutions can be found even for those problems which seem most intractable.'

⊙ Keep going. Perhaps an underrated attribute, but Mandela required extraordinary stamina to navigate the many obstacles that confronted him. In that time he was also prepared to admit his mistakes and learn from them for the next time. The final paragraph of *Long Walk to Freedom* reads: 'I have walked that long road to freedom. I have tried not to falter; I have made missteps along the way. But I have discovered the secret that after climbing a great hill, one only finds that there are many more hills to climb. I have taken a moment here to rest, to steal a view of the glorious vista that surrounds me, to look back on the distance I have come. But I can rest only for a moment, for with freedom come responsibilities, and I dare not linger, for my long walk is not yet ended.'

'Nelson Mandela was more than one of the greatest leaders of our time. He was one of our greatest teachers.'

BAN-KI MOON, UN SECRETARY-GENERAL, 2013

Those Who Inspired Mandela

'My inspiration are men and women who have emerged throughout the globe, and who have chosen the world as the theatre of their operations and who fight socio-economic conditions which do not help towards the advancement of humanity wherever that occurs. Men and women who fight the suppression of the human voice, who fight disease, illiteracy, ignorance, poverty and hunger. Some are known, others are not.'

NELSON MANDELA IN ADDRESS TO THE LONDON SCHOOL OF ECONOMICS, 2000

On one memorable day in 1997, Nelson Mandela (who at the time was President) met the Spice Girls (then one of the world's most successful pop bands). With a wry look in his eye, he commented: 'These are my heroes. This is one of the greatest moments in my life.' While Sporty, Scary, Ginger, Baby and Posh undoubtedly appealed to many men around the world, it is fair to assume that in the grand scheme of things they held nothing higher than a lower mid-table position among those who helped mould Mandela.

As the quotation at the beginning of this section suggests, he was a man far more interested in those who put themselves out to improve the conditions of others. While he undoubtedly understood the power of celebrity (see page 102), it was not one's level of fame by which he judged the value of a life. Instead, he most admired those who combine conscience with action. On that basis, he found inspiration in all sorts of unlikely places, including from those whose politics were far removed from his own.

For instance, we know that he avidly read *Commando*, the memoirs of the Boer guerrilla, Deneys Reitz, who ultimately served as Deputy Prime Minister in the government of Jan Smuts in the early 1940s. Reitz's experiences offered Mandela practical lessons as to the nature of guerrilla warfare against a theoretically stronger enemy and thus Reitz's narrative served, against expectations, as an inspirational story of sorts.

Similarly, Mandela was something of a devotee of the writings of Carl von Clausewitz, a German–Prussian army man who made his name as one of the great military theorists of the late-eighteenth and early-nineteenth centuries. Never underestimating the need for militarily-sound strategy in his own ideological fight, Mandela also developed an interest in Luis Taruc, a Filipino communist guerrilla insurgent who served a twelve-year prison sentence for his underground activities in the 1940s and 1950s.

There are, of course, other more obviously relevant figures whose lives we know Mandela studied. He was certainly well versed in the stories of tribal figures who battled colonial hegemony. In the unpublished sequel to *Long Walk to Freedom* he set out a few names from this roll-call of honour whom he described as being 'in the forefront of the wars of resistance' and worthy of 'respect and admiration'.

> ⊙ Autshumao, a leader of the Khoikhoi who in the seventeenth century acted as an interpreter for European traders and settlers but who eventually waged war against the Dutch and was ultimately imprisoned on Robben Island by them.

- ⊙ Maqoma of the Rharhabe, a Xhosa leader who fought against the British in the nineteenth century until he was sent to Robben Island at the age of seventy-three, where he died two years later, reputedly of 'old age and dejection'.
- ⊙ Bambatha, a Zulu chief who led a 1906 protest against a British-imposed poll tax that soon developed into a full-scale uprising. Bambatha himself lost his life in the rout that was the Battle of Mome Gorge.
- ⊙ Cetshwayo, the King of the Zulu Kingdom who led his forces into war against the invading British in 1879. He secured a landmark victory against the British at the Battle of Isandhlwana, despite far inferior weaponry.
- ⊙ Mampuru of the Pedis, the leader of the Pedi in the Transvaal who fought first against the Boers before turning his attentions to the British, all while engaged in a dynastic battle for power that spanned a period of several decades.
- ⊙ Moshoeshoe, the founder of Basutoland, which evolved into the modern state of Lesotho. He successfully defended his territory against both the Boers and the British for the duration of his life.

In an address to the US Congress that he delivered in 1990, Mandela pointed to some of the giant figures from US history whom he had come to hear of and admire through the literature he had read. This too is an illuminating list. Unsurprisingly, he cited the likes of George Washington and Thomas Jefferson, Founding Fathers of the American nation and pioneers of modern democracy. Abraham Lincoln was mentioned too, not least for his role in the abolition of slavery. Martin Luther King, Jr, champion of the civil rights movement who ultimately gave his life for the cause, was predictably there, as was the Jamaican-born Marcus Garvey, pioneer of Pan-Africanism (an ideological movement that sees the histories and destinies of all African peoples worldwide as fundamentally intertwined).

There were several less familiar names as well, indicative of Mandela's deep historical reading. He spoke, for instance, of the nineteenth-century abolitionist, John Brown, along with Frederick Douglass, a former slave who became a well-known campaigner for social reform in the Victorian era. Also, W. E. B. Du Bois, an African-American academic and civil rights campaigner whose life straddled the latter part of the nineteenth century and a large part of the twentieth, and Sojourner Truth, a former slave who previously went under the name of Isabella Baumfree before reinventing herself as a campaigning voice for abolitionism and female rights.

We also know that Mandela made a study of the teachings and activities of Booker T. Washington. Washington had risen from lowly slave roots to become the dominant African-American figure in the late nineteenth and early twentieth centuries, serving as a sounding board for both President Theodore Roosevelt and his successor,

William Taft. George Padmore, a noted writer and Pan-Africanist in the 1930s, 1940s and 1950s, is another whose writings were influential on Mandela. Similarly, those of Kwame Nkrumah, the man who secured independence for Ghana (previously the Gold Coast) from the UK in 1957. He too espoused Pan-Africanism and was, like Mandela, by inclination drawn towards Marxism. In further echoes of Mandela, Nkrumah endured prolonged periods in prison as the colonial government sought to counter his activism. However, his influence only went so far with Mandela who, once head of state, followed a vastly different style of leadership to the authoritarianism Nkrumah adopted until he was overthrown in a coup.

THE INDIAN CONNECTION

It is often assumed that Mahatma Gandhi, the man who brought the curtain down on British rule in India once and for all in 1947, was a major influence on Mandela. He was, after all, the most famous civil rights and freedom campaigner of the generation that preceded Mandela's. Though there were several decades between the two men (Gandhi was born in Gujarat, India, in 1869, almost fifty years before Mandela took his first breaths), there were a number of marked parallels between their lives – not least their fundamental belief in a common humanity.

Both were also lawyers and used the legal system to challenge injustice. Having been called to the Bar in London, Gandhi went on to forge his early career in South Africa, initially providing legal representation to Muslim Indian traders based in Pretoria. He spent twenty-one years in the country, from 1893 until 1914, and experienced many of the 'thousand indignities' that would so enflame Mandela in years to come. On one occasion, for instance, Gandhi was thrown off a train for refusing to leave the first class section on account of his race (a case he took up with and won against the rail company involved). On another occasion, he was beaten up for refusing to cede his seat to a European traveller and he was regularly denied access to certain hotels too. Such treatment made him increasingly alert to injustice until he decided to become an activist himself.

Gandhi campaigned for reforms to laws denying Indians voting rights and was instrumental in the birth of the Indian Congress in South Africa. In 1906, he co-ordinated mass demonstrations against an Act requiring the registration of all Indian citizens. He urged his fellow protestors to defy the law and accept the consequences – arrest, imprisonment and physical intimidation – without flinching. It was the first practical demonstration of his evolving philosophy of *Satyagraha*, or non-violent protest, which would inform Mandela's own approach to protest. In Gandhi's words: 'Passive resistance is a method of securing rights by personal suffering. It is the reverse of resistance by arms.'

Both Gandhi and Mandela would endure spells of incarceration at Fort Prison in Johannesburg, the former in 1908 and the latter in 1956 and 1962. Both used hunger strikes in prison as a means of protest and Gandhi's ghost was certainly evident in the 1952 Defiance Campaign, which was jointly run by the ANC and the South African Indian Congress.

Perhaps more surprisingly, Mandela could even find justification for his adoption of armed protest in the words of his Indian forefather. In 1938, for instance, Gandhi had written that violence was better than the 'emasculation of a whole race'. On another occasion, he argued:

I have been repeating over and over again that he who cannot protect himself or his nearest and dearest or their honour by non-violently facing death may and ought to do so by violently dealing with the oppressor.

Mandela spoke glowingly of his predecessor at the unveiling of the Mahatma Gandhi Memorial in Pietermaritzburg in 1993:

Today as we strive to achieve a date for the first democratic elections in this country, the legacy of Gandhiji has an immediate relevance. He negotiated in good faith and without bitterness. But when the oppressor reneged he returned to mass resistance.

In 1979 Mandela had received the Jawaharlal Nehru Award for International Understanding. As he was in jail, Oliver Tambo accepted it on his behalf and said the following:

...the striking role of India in the development of the struggle for national and social liberation in South Africa has its firm roots in the early campaigns led by Mahatma Gandhi in that country, coupled with the continuing and active interest he took in the South African situation. All South Africans have particular cause to honour and remember the man, who was in our midst for twenty-one years and went on to enter the history books as the Father of Free India. His imprint on the course of the South African struggle is indelible.

However, in an interview with Ahmed Kathrada in the 1990s, Mandela would say: 'Nehru was really my hero.' Why might that have been? Certainly, during his time in South Africa, Gandhi was heavily focussed on securing rights

for Indians rather than blacks. So, for instance, in 1906 he urged that Indians be allowed to enlist in the British forces to help put down the Zulu Bambatha Uprising in Natal. It was a move he hoped would propel forward his campaign for full citizenship for Indians but was one hardly likely to endear him to Mandela, that student of history.

Born in 1889, mid-way between Gandhi and Mandela, Jawaharlal Nehru was British-educated and, like the other two, a lawyer. Politically, he was a democrat, a secularist and a socialist who served as India's Prime Minister from independence in 1947 until his death in 1964. He was also a pragmatist in the best sense of the word. One of Mandela's career-defining addresses – his 'No Easy Walk to Freedom' speech in 1953 – owes its title to a Nehru quotation.

Having achieved his dream of an independent India, Nehru was well attuned to the struggle ongoing in Africa and eager to lend his support. In 1955 he had told the Bandung Conference (a meeting of African and Asian states held in Indonesia):

There is nothing more terrible than the infinite tragedy of Africa in the past few hundred years... But unfortunately, in a different sense, even now the tragedy of Africa is greater than that of any other continent, whether it is racial or political. It is up to Asia to help Africa to the best of her ability because we are sister continents.

Nehru, then, was far more a practical 'brother-in-arms' to Mandela than Gandhi – who was assassinated before Mandela was well known on the global stage – could ever really be.

In the speech Oliver Tambo delivered for Mandela to accept the 1979 Nehru Award on his behalf, the appreciation he felt for Nehru was evident:

If Mahatma Gandhi started and fought his heroic struggle in South Africa and India, Jawaharlal Nehru was to continue it in Asia, Africa and internationally. In 1946, India broke trade relations with South Africa – the first country to do so. In the same year, at the First Session of the United Nations General Assembly, the Indian Government sharply raised the question of racial discrimination in South Africa – again the first country to take this action.

But Mandela's admiration was most clearly voiced in the Rajiv Gandhi Foundation Lecture he delivered in 1995:

Jawaharlal Nehru taught us that the right to a roof over one's head and affordable services, a job and reasonable income, education and health facilities is more than just a bonus to democracy. It is the essence of democracy itself; the essence of human rights.

Be a People Person

'He can be sharp. He can be moody, but he is naturally very warm. And he fits into the leadership. He has the ability to conduct himself as a leader.'

WALTER SISULU, INTERVIEWED BY JOHN CARLIN
FOR PBS *FRONTLINE*, 1999

M andela's almost unique status on the global stage was achieved in part by his natural propensity to charm. Few who met him who weren't his political foes were ever less than complimentary about him as a man (and even some of his sworn enemies were swept away by his personality). He was renowned for his warmth, generosity and good humour allied to an endearingly mischievous streak. It is an image that in turn ensured his reputation among those who never met him personally. There are few public figures who have unified people so apparently effortlessly and fewer still who have used their people skills so selflessly. So just what was it that made him such a 'people person'?

Some of it is undoubtedly the result of an imponderable natural charisma. He was, even in old age, a fine looking man with a warm smile and an open and welcoming demeanour. He was also said to have an exceptional memory for faces that ensured those who met him more than once were made to feel special.

He had an air of humility that many other political figures would do well to learn from. In the unpublished sequel to *Long Walk to Freedom*, he reflected: 'There is universal respect and even admiration for those who are humble and simple by nature, and who have absolute confidence in all human beings irrespective of their social status.' And as his great friend, writer and political activist Nadine Gordimer, has noted, he had 'the capacity to live for others'.

He also prided himself on his ability to integrate with people from all walks of life. He himself had variously been a member of tribal nobility, a rare black presence in largely white educational establishments, a rural boy in the big city, an outlaw, a prisoner and a president, so it is perhaps little surprise that he developed a chameleon-like ability to fit in wherever he was. But it was a skill he had early on. Looking back on his time on the run in 1962, for instance, he spoke with pride of how he was able to forge links with contacts from a variety of backgrounds, whether they were 'Muslims in the Cape... sugar-workers in Natal... [or] factory workers in Port Elizabeth'.

Linked to this talent for building relationships was a willingness to see the good in others. 'Let us remind ourselves,' he said in 2008, 'that it is ordinary people – men and women, boys and girls – that make the world a special place.' He acknowledged that there would be those who felt he was sometimes too quick to see the good but that was, he said, a criticism he could bear as he believed his approach yielded the greater rewards. Addressing parliament in 2004 to mark ten years of democracy, he told the assembly: 'We signal that good can be achieved amongst human beings who are prepared to trust, prepared to believe in the goodness of people.'

In addition, he had the good grace to overlook others' frailties, while freely acknowledging his own. It is an attitude perhaps best expressed in a letter he sent to Winnie in 1979:

> In real life we deal, not with gods, but with ordinary humans like ourselves: men and women who are full of contradictions, who are stable and fickle, strong and weak, famous and infamous, people in whose bloodstream the muckworm battles daily with potent pesticides.

Finally, he had the ability to bring people together by hitting upon the common cause that unites them. A skill writ large in the story of the overthrow of apartheid. In his own words:

> I remind people again and again that the liberation struggle was not a battle against any one group or colour, but a fight against a system of repression. At every opportunity, I said all South Africans must now unite and join hands and say we are one country, one nation, one people, marching together into the future.

Choose Your Friends Wisely

'He has a knack of doing just the right thing and
being able to carry it off with aplomb.'

ARCHBISHOP DESMOND TUTU, INTERVIEWED BY
JOHN CARLIN FOR PBS *FRONTLINE*, 1999

While a 'man of the people', Mandela always had the good sense to surround himself with a circle of friends whom he trusted implicitly, even when they had not always seen eye to eye. He was no fan of sycophancy nor of people pursuing self-serving agendas of their own. If the post-prison Mandela appeared at times a gentle and lovable giant, he maintained throughout his life an admirably pragmatic attitude to those around him.

Given the size of the challenges he took on, he was quick to realize that most were more easily overcome in the company of allies. At the political level, this sometimes required compromise. As a young upstart in the ANC, for instance, he argued for a distinct separation from other protest bodies such as the South African Indian Congress and the Communist Party. However, over time he realized that there were mutual benefits to fostering closer relations. As an example, he came to believe that the ANC was fighting not only for equality in race but in class too, providing an obvious tie-in with the Communists. 'I had discovered that the Communists were genuine allies and they had no ulterior motive,' he reflected in 1993. In addition, he recognized that other groups had organizational strengths from which the ANC could benefit. By 1950, he was much more open to pursuing alliances as long as the ANC retained its overall independence.

He realized that it was OK to let your friends do some of your work for you – a pragmatic approach he maintained in the battles he waged in the post-apartheid era, too. We can see this most clearly in his campaign for AIDS awareness. He told *Time* magazine in 1990: 'These problems cannot be tackled on personal basis, they can only be dealt with through a collective effort. I will not be acting as an individual. I will be acting as a member of a team.'

He perhaps valued loyalty above all other traits and kept his most trusted friends close over whole lifetimes. In letters written during his prison years he commented variously that, 'It is always a source of immense strength to enjoy the support of powerful and faithful friends' and that 'I have always regarded friendship as something very precious'.

In his post-prison years, he was knocked in some quarters for relationships he kept up with a number of controversial global leaders who had supported him financially and morally during the dark days prior to 1990 (see page 176). Few things have so obviously stung him as that criticism. He told a joint press conference with US President Bill Clinton in 1998: 'Those South Africans who have berated me for being loyal to our friends, literally, they can go and throw themselves in a pool.'

Along with loyalty, he also prized intelligence and honesty, even when it came in the form of constructive criticism. 'I like friends who have independent minds,' he said in the unpublished biography he wrote on Robben Island, 'because they tend to make you see problems from all angles.' And in an interview with Ahmed Kathrada in 1996, he said 'I believe in surrounding myself with strong characters who will tell me when I am wrong...'

Inevitably, perhaps the greatest friendships of his life were forged in the heat of the anti-apartheid battle. Kathrada, a fellow Rivonia defendant, was himself one of Mandela's closest allies. Also important were Albert Luthuli – President of the ANC from 1952 until 1967 and the Nobel Peace Prize-winner in 1960 – though his relationship with Mandela was not always smooth, and Anton Lembede, who died in 1947 aged thirty-three but not before he had co-founded the ANC Youth League and exerted significant influence on his younger colleague. Arguably his most important friendships, though, were with Walter Sisulu and Oliver Tambo.

PROFILE: Walter Sisulu

Sisulu and Mandela were comrades-in-arms and soul mates so that after Sisulu died on 5 May 2003, Mandela said: 'His absence has carved a void. A part of me is gone.'

Sisulu was born on 18 May 1912 in Engcobo in the Transkei. He was born to a black mother and a white father, a colonial administrator who was absent from his son's childhood. Walter had a tough upbringing and for large parts of it was raised by his grandmother and an uncle. When Sisulu was fifteen, his uncle died and he was forced to leave school and start work. Over time, he gravitated to Johannesburg and lived in the impoverished Orlando township in the Soweto area of the city.

In 1940 he became a member of the ANC and met Mandela the following year. Sisulu was at the time an estate agent and was able to provide Mandela with contacts in the legal world. Their acquaintanceship would soon bloom into something far more profound. In years to come, Mandela would describe Sisulu as 'my friend, my brother, my keeper and my comrade'. When Sisulu married his bride, Albertina, in 1944, Mandela was best man at their wedding.

That same year, Sisulu served as treasurer and sat on the executive committee – along with Mandela, Oliver Tambo, Ashley Mda and Anton Lembede – of the newly formed ANC Youth League. He was an increasingly key figure in the ANC, renowned for his abilities as a political networker. He became its Secretary-General in 1949, staying in the post until 1954. In 1952 he was instrumental to the organization of the Defiance Campaign and from 1961 had a prominent planning role with the ANC's militant arm, Umkhonto we Sizwe (MK). He was also a member of the South African Communist Party.

As his public profile rose, so did his problems with the government. He, like Mandela, was repeatedly arrested, imprisoned and banned from attending public gatherings.

In the end, the decision was made that he should operate from underground and he spent a considerable time building relations with allies abroad. Arrested after the Rivonia raid in 1963, he was convicted the following year and sentenced to twenty-five years in jail.

In his years on Robben Island, he was part of the informal 'behind-bars university' that operated there, educating fellow prisoners on the history of the ANC from its inception. Albertina, meanwhile, played a vital role in those years, acting as a go-between for the ANC leaders in prison and those in exile. When Mandela began talks with the government in the late 1980s, he pushed hard for the release of fellow political prisoners and Sisulu was freed in 1989.

In July 1991 he was elected Deputy President of the ANC to Mandela's President. He stayed in the post until he retired from frontline politics in 1994, following the successful conclusion of democratic elections. He died in 2003.

One of his greatest achievements was to help Mandela maintain focus. As Mandela once commented: 'By ancestry, I was born to rule. Xhamela [Sisulu's tribal name] helped me understand that my real vocation was to be a servant of the people.' At Sisulu's funeral, Mandela gave a heartfelt eulogy to his erstwhile comrade. He described a figure who was courageous and quietly self-confident, and who had the 'clarity of vision' that marked him out as a leader. He was, too, someone who would not ask of others that which he was not prepared to do himself.

Given the stresses and strains of the arena in which they were operating, it is hardly surprising that there were on occasions tensions between the two men and Mandela admitted to finding Sisulu sometimes 'vexing and frustrating'. As he explained:

At times the clashes were so sharp that some of the comrades were taken aback. Such incidents happened before we went to prison, while we were in prison and even after we came out of prison. We had grown up and lived in the strong culture of vigorous debate in the ANC. None of these sharp exchanges were allowed to harm our friendship and the bonds that held us in the ANC.

Furthermore, Mandela considered Sisulu blessed with a quality that allowed him to always see the good in others. He also admired Sisulu's capacity to listen to others and to encourage them to explore ideas. Even after Xhamela died, Mandela kept up his connection with the Sisulu family when he employed his son, a journalist called Zwelakhe, as his press secretary. Reflecting on his own mortality, Mandela said:

I now know that when my time comes, Walter will be there to meet me, and I am almost certain he will hold out an enrolment form to register me into the ANC with that world, cajoling me with one of his favourite songs…

PROFILE: Oliver Tambo

Oliver Reginald Kaizana Tambo was born in Cape Province on 27 October 1917 and brought up in the Christian faith. His father, though a traditionalist, was keen that his son should receive a Western-style schooling and so Tambo entered formal education aged six. Just as Mandela received the name 'Nelson' from his school, so Tambo was called 'Oliver' by his teacher.

Also in common with Mandela, Tambo was a keen sportsman, as well as being a talented musician and a very able scholar. His hopes of studying medicine were thwarted on the basis of his race, so he took a degree in science at Fort Hare, where he met Mandela. Together they were prominent on the university's political scene.

After securing his degree, Tambo began a diploma in higher education but was expelled from the university for his political activities (specifically, a programme of non-cooperation in response to a dispute over the use of a tennis court). He subsequently became a teacher at his old school, St Peter's Secondary School in Rosettenville, Johannesburg. With the three of them based in the city by the early 1940s, Mandela, Sisulu and Tambo met regularly together, along with other intellectuals and leading figures from the ANC.

Tambo qualified as a lawyer and set up a landmark firm with Mandela. In 1944 he was one of the founding members of the ANC Youth League, becoming its first National Secretary. Four years later he joined the ANC National Executive and in 1955 he took over as party

Secretary-General in succession to Sisulu. The following year he married Adelaide Tshukudo, although the wedding nearly didn't happen as Tambo was charged with treason (of which he would later be acquitted).

He served as Deputy President of the ANC from 1958–67, despite a five-year banning order by the government in 1959 restricting his ability to speak in public. He was ANC Acting President from 1967 until 1977, and then its President until 1991, at which point he took up the post of National Chairman. Yet from the early 1960s, Tambo lived in exile, charged with keeping alive the ANC's message internationally. He and his family were based in Muswell Hill in London until he finally returned to his homeland in December 1990. He had suffered a stroke the year before that had rather diminished his powers. Fittingly, though, he was received as a hero for seeing through the task of holding the ANC together while so many of his colleagues festered in prison cells.

Although now a free man, Mandela refused to take the top job with the ANC immediately, instead insisting that Tambo retain the role for the time being. Tambo may not have been a great orator but was, like Mandela, noted for his natural charm and his willingness to listen to others. He died on 24 April 1993.

In an address to the ANC in 1997, Mandela paid tribute to him with the following words: 'Oliver Tambo was like no one else; a brother and a friend to me. He enriched my own life and intellect; and neither I nor indeed this country can forget this colossus of our history.'

Deliver the
Message

'A freedom fighter must take every opportunity
to make his case to the people.'

NELSON MANDELA, *LONG WALK TO FREEDOM*

When Mandela is not being compared to Gandhi, he is most regularly likened to Martin Luther King among the pantheon of modern giants. Yet where King was, perhaps alongside Winston Churchill and John F. Kennedy, the pre-eminent orator of the twentieth century, public speaking was never Mandela's greatest forte. And still he managed to convey his message of social change with unrivalled success.

As this book goes some way to showing, his was not a career devoid of memorable lines and finely turned phrases. Nonetheless, a layman may struggle to come up with his 'I have a dream' moment or his 'We will fight them on the beaches' equivalent. His vocal tone, idiosyncratic intonation and particular quirks (such as a fondness for using the 'royal we') did not always contribute to oratorical triumphs.

He became wary of blood-and-thunder speeches early on. In a 1953 address to the ANC (Transvaal) Congress, he said:

Long speeches, the shaking of fists, the banging of tables and strongly worded resolutions out of touch with the objective conditions do not bring about mass action and can do a great deal of harm to the organization and the struggle we serve.

It was a subject still concerning him in a 1970 letter to Winnie:

There is a stage in the life of every social reformer when he will thunder on platforms primarily to relieve himself of the scraps of undigested information that has accumulated in his head; an attempt to impress crowds rather than to start a calm and simple exposition of principles and ideas whose universal truth is made evident by personal experience and deeper study.

So there was a conscious rejection of oratory for its own sake. In 1993 he told an interviewer that he avoided rabble-rousing speeches as he had concluded that the masses prefer to see somebody speak in what he termed a 'responsible manner'. He described how success in politics relies on your ability to take people into your confidence and to state your views openly, clearly, calmly and politely. His experience as a prisoner also informed his attitude, as he revealed in his closing address to the XI International AIDS Conference held in Durban in 2000:

It is never my custom to use words lightly. If twenty-seven years in prison have done anything to us, it was to use the silence of solitude to make us understand how precious words are and how real speech is in its impact on the way people live and die.

It is an intriguing fact that some of his most important speeches were not delivered in front of enthusiastic crowds of supporters but within the relative discipline of the courtroom. As a lawyer, he was a notable performer in that arena, and so he proved to be as a defendant too. In particular, his trial in 1962 and, two years later, the Rivonia trial were vital forums in which he communicated the case against apartheid.

He enjoyed certain rhetorical flourishes – his speeches and writings, for instance, often used the language of struggle and challenge (one need only think of his choice of title for his autobiography). But in the dock he relied upon simple, uncluttered language to deliver potent messages, thriving in his role as a 'symbol of justice in the court of the oppressor'. Consider the eloquence of this statement he made to the court in Pretoria in 1962:

That the will of the people is the basis of the authority of government is a principle universally acknowledged as sacred throughout the civilized world, and constitutes the basic foundations of freedom and justice. It is understandable why citizens, who have the vote as well as the right to direct representation in the country's governing bodies, should be morally and legally bound by the laws governing the country.

At the Rivonia trial, he delivered arguably the most potent oration of his life, as he spoke of the 'ideal for which I am prepared to die' (explored in more detail on page 101).

He should also be considered a highly skilled manipulator of his public image. If his public speaking was not always the most polished, he was never less than a remarkable performer in public. This is not to say that he ever wilfully put on an act to deceive. Indeed, he once wrote of his fears that his public image did not tally with reality:

One issue that deeply worried me in prison was the false image that I unwittingly projected to the outside world – of being regarded as a saint. I never was one, even on the basis of an earthly definition of a saint as a sinner who keeps on trying.

Nonetheless, his 'public performances' – marked by that potent combination of natural warmth, self-effacing wit, calm determination, an almost other-worldly air of tranquillity – helped deliver his messages time and again when his public speaking alone might not have sufficed. All of which is to say, we listened to Mandela perhaps less for his oratorical skills than for the sense that he was a figure who warranted being listened to.

THE RIVONIA TRIAL

The Rivonia Trial was a key moment in the life of Mandela and for the entire anti-apartheid movement. It provided a platform from which Mandela and his co-defendants could convincingly set out the case against the national government, with precious little regard for their own welfare. It cost them decades of their lives (and for all they knew at the time, might have seen them executed) but it also cast them as figures of moral authority at home and abroad. Without such stature, we can only ponder what direction the anti-apartheid movement might have taken.

So what were the origins of this extraordinary episode that proved so influential in the formation of the Mandela legend? The story starts in Rivonia, a suburb of Johannesburg, in 1961. In August of that year the Liliesleaf farm was secretly purchased on behalf of the South African Communist Party (SACP). It was intended to be used as a safe house by underground activists from the SACP and other organizations. Some of its buildings became printing houses from where anti-government literature was distributed and it was also the site for the first test broadcastings of Freedom Radio, the ANC's own dedicated station that proved a potent weapon in the liberation struggle. The farm is also now acknowledged as having been the spiritual birthplace of the MK military wing of the ANC.

Fast-forward to August 1962, when Mandela was arrested at Howick, a town on the road between Durban and Johannesburg. He had recently returned from a meeting of the Pan-African Freedom Movement for Central and East Africa in Addis Ababa, Ethiopia. In due course, he would be sentenced to five years in prison.

Mandela had previously spent time in Rivonia with a great many of the other leading ANC figures, using the farm as a base from which to plan their campaigns of action. He was aware that there were incriminating documents on site and so he smuggled out a message to Liliesleaf that his papers should be destroyed. However, his colleagues took the decision that they were too important to be disposed of so instead they buried them in a coal shed.

On 11 July 1963, the police launched a raid on the Rivonia base in search of Walter Sisulu, whom they had been tipped off was in hiding there. Instead, they uncovered a meeting of the High Command of the MK, along with plans for Operation Mayibuye, a proposed guerrilla insurgency against the apartheid government that had been formulated by fellow activists Govan Mbeki and Joe Slovo. All those present were arrested and held separately under the ninety-day detention laws.

A few months later, Mandela – already in prison – was implicated in the case after his papers were found. The trial of eleven defendants began on 26 November 1963 and was restarted a week later with a revised indictment. One of the defendants, Bob Hepple, was removed from the indictment after he agreed to testify for the prosecution. The remainder were accused of the following offences:

- Recruiting persons for training in the preparation and use of explosives and in guerrilla warfare for the purpose of violent revolution and committing acts of sabotage.
- Conspiring to commit the aforementioned acts and to aid foreign military units when they invaded the Republic.
- Acting in these ways to further the objects of Communism.
- Soliciting and receiving money for these purposes from sympathisers in Algeria, Tunisia, Ethiopia, Liberia, Nigeria and elsewhere.

In June 1964, the verdicts were returned. Lionel 'Rusty' Bernstein was acquitted, as was James Kantor, who had been Mandela's defence lawyer but was himself put under arrest after his brother-in-law, Harold Wolpe, had earlier escaped from custody along with Arthur Goldreich in the aftermath of the raid. Each of the other defendants – Mandela, Sisulu, Denis Goldberg, Ahmed Kathrada, Govan Mbeki, Raymond Mhlaba, Andrew Mlangeni and Elias Motsoaledi – was given a life sentence. Mandela, as we know, would not emerge into the light for twenty-seven years.

What could have been a fatal blow for the anti-apartheid movement was, nonetheless, turned around by the dignity and eloquence of those in the dock, and especially Mandela. His speech to the court made on 20 April 1964 as he faced the prospect of capital punishment, was not only a rallying cry for all those already dedicated to the cause but won for it legions of new supporters too:

I have dedicated myself to this struggle of the African people. I have fought against White domination, and I have fought against Black domination. I have cherished the ideal of a democratic and free society in which all persons live together in harmony and with equal opportunities. It is an ideal which I hope to live for and to achieve. But, if needs be, it is an ideal for which I am prepared to die.

The course of history was set.

Harness
Celebrity

'I didn't know that I would meet a British princess.'

MANDELA ON MEETING PRINCESS DIANA, 1997

M andela had a sure grasp of the power of celebrity – both his own and that of others. Some accused him of having sometimes had his head turned by celebrity after his release from prison. Having spent twenty-seven years cooped up, one could hardly blame him. But the truth of the matter is rather more nuanced.

During his incarceration, celebrity ensured that he and the anti-apartheid cause were not forgotten. For instance, in 1985 Stevie Wonder received an Oscar for his song 'I Just Called to Say I Love You' and dedicated the award to Mandela, the song receiving a ban in South Africa for his troubles. Then came Mandela's seventieth birthday concert (see page 140), which used other big-name pop stars to bring his plight to the attention of a youthful global audience.

After his release, he was able to use his own celebrity to leverage attention for the causes that mattered to him. Whether it was through meeting the Spice Girls or Princess Diana, buddying up with Bill Clinton, being kissed by Beyoncé or hugged by Bono, his work to fight AIDS and improve children's educational opportunities received coverage that money could never hope to buy.

In the case of Oprah Winfrey, who famously interviewed him in 2000, their joint celebrity was directly responsible for the birth of a high-profile initiative. In an interview with the writer Marianne Schanll, Winfrey explained the inspiration behind the Oprah Winfrey Leadership Academy for Girls, which opened in 2007 near Johannesburg to provide opportunities for girls from impoverished backgrounds.

Being in Nelson Mandela's living room, literally sitting in his living room in 2002 when I had gone over to do something called Christmas Kindness... That's why I was sitting in Nelson's Mandela's living room – he invited me to stay at his house while we were going village to village bringing gifts to children. And we were having a conversation about what's going to really make a difference in the world. And he said, changing poverty – you can't change the world unless you change poverty, and I said, you can't change poverty unless you educate people, and that's the way through. And I said, 'I would really love to build a school someday for South Africa.' And I really was thinking, ah, someday, that will be the thing that I do when I retire or whatever. And he said, 'You want to build a school!' – he got up, literally jumped up, called the Minister of Education and set me up on the phone with the Minister of Education. And in a conversation with the Minister of Education, by the end of that evening, we were told to come over to the house. So that's how it all started.

Wear It Well

'A president should always wear a suit, a white shirt,
a tie and a hat. My uncle dresses disgracefully.
He dresses like a drunkard.'

NELSON MANDELA QUOTING HIS NEPHEW

M andela was a man who always prided himself on his sartorial elegance. For the large part of his public life, he favoured neat tailored suits, shirts and ties. He was, after all, someone who knew that what you wore conveyed a message. If you wanted to be taken seriously, you needed to dress seriously.

His early years in Johannesburg – and particularly in fashionable Sophiatown – were important in defining his Western-influenced style. At his trial in 1962, though, he made an immediate impact by turning up on the first day in a leopard-skin *kaross* – a type of traditional Xhosa robe. He would later describe how he felt as if he was 'the embodiment of African nationalism'.

One of the great hardships of his subsequent prison years was the imposition of a uniform. In particular, there was a rule that said black prisoners (unlike their white or coloured counterparts) were not allowed to wear long trousers, being issued instead with khaki shorts. Such an affront was it to Mandela that he formally protested and further showed his dissatisfaction by, for instance, refusing to walk at the demanded pace and declining to call warders *baas* (master).

Once out of prison, the smart suits returned as he navigated South Africa's passage to democracy. Then in the build-up to his inauguration as President in 1994, something remarkable happened. He took to wearing a style of shirt that became synonymous not only with him but with South Africa as a whole. It would come to be known as a Madiba shirt, Madiba being the clan nickname by which Mandela is popularly known.

So what exactly is the look? In short, the Madiba shirt is made from a brightly coloured fabric and worn loose and flowing. Mandela customarily wore it untucked with shoes and slacks, buttoned at the cuffs and neck but without a tie or jacket. The bold prints had a sense of joyousness that a staid suit simply cannot rival. It is, however, by no means a look that everyone can carry off, with many having tried and failed. Nonetheless, the trend quickly took hold and Madiba shirts are now a staple in clothes shops up and down South Africa.

Given the impact it has had (and the money to be made from selling it), credit for creating the look has been hotly contested. There are three main claimants. The first is Yusuf Surtee, a designer whose store provided Mandela with clothing dating back to his incarceration when Mandela needed outfits suitable for attending political negotiations. Surtee claimed he created the Madiba shirt after Mandela requested a shirt like one that Indonesia's President Suharto had given him on an official visit after his release.

Then there is Desre Buirski, who tells the story of

how she made a silk shirt featuring an eye-catching fish design. On 7 May 1994 she handed it to one of Mandela's bodyguards during a visit to a synagogue in Cape Town. Sensibly, she also slipped her contact details into the pocket. A fortnight later, Mandela wore it to the dress rehearsal for the opening of the first democratically elected parliament in the country's history. Subsequently, Buirski was commissioned to make further pieces for the President, supplying him with well over a hundred shirts in the ensuing years.

The final claimant is Sonwabile Ndamase, who was introduced to the great man after Mandela's release from prison in 1990 and began creating shirts for him using locally sourced Batik (a type of fabric that originated in Indonesia). He claimed he created the style as a way to thank Mandela for his 'magnanimous bravery'. 'I am not disputing that others have designed shirts for him,' he has said, 'but I was the first to do it.'

According to Buirski, Mandela preferred his shirts in earthier tones but for many, it is the brighter colours that best suit an item of apparel that has come to encapsulate the Rainbow Nation. Whoever created it, the Madiba shirt is a powerful symbol of the fusion of old and new Africa, its daring and colourful designs suggestive of a nation aware of its history but self-confident and eager to embrace what the world has to offer. And nobody wore it quite like Nelson.

'Without doubt one of the best
dressed men in South Africa.'

ADELAIDE TAMBO, INTERVIEWED BY
JOHN CARLIN FOR PBS FRONTLINE, 1999

Yet even an icon will have his critics. When it comes to Madiba shirts, one of them is Archbishop Desmond Tutu, who has argued that Mandela looked 'more elegant and dignified' in a suit. However, Jay Naidoo, a cabinet minister during the Mandela presidency, was quoted as saying: 'That is a little rich coming from a man in a dress.'

Show Bravery in Adversity

'I learned that courage was not the absence of fear, but the triumph over it. I felt fear myself more times than I can remember, but I hid it behind a mask of boldness. The brave man is not he who does not feel afraid, but he who conquers that fear.'

NELSON MANDELA, *LONG WALK TO FREEDOM*

M andela was not the first to have noted that bravery is not the absence of fear but a willingness to confront it. However, few can claim to have shown bravery so comprehensively in their own lives.

The death of his father when Mandela was still a child forced him to grow up more quickly than he might otherwise have done. He was presented with a brutal choice: crumble or face down the worst that life could throw at him. That he chose the latter option set the pattern for the rest of his life. He would in due course suffer the loss of other relatives, including his own children, and close friends, sometimes in the most heart-breaking of circumstances. The death of his mother in 1968 and his son Thembi in a car crash the following year coincided with his imprisonment and a refusal by the authorities to let him attend either funeral. That his spirit was not crushed by these events alone is testament to his fortitude.

Yet his courage in dealing with the brickbats thrown at him by fate was always accompanied by an even rarer willingness to actively put himself in the path of difficulty in order to achieve his wider aims. Take the refusal to renege on his principles that cost him his chance of graduating from Fort Hare when he knew that life would be much simpler if he accepted what he regarded as the unjust behaviour of the university administration. In the grand scheme of things, the issues at hand were low-level but it was not a compromise that he could make in good faith. So he took his stand, accepted the consequences and moved on.

Such experiences prepared him well for the many years of non-violent dissent that lay ahead, when protestors knew they faced the threat of imprisonment and officially-sanctioned violence. The 1952 Campaign of Defiance Mandela coordinated was distinctly Gandhi-ist in its approach so it is worth looking at what Gandhi himself said about his particular brand of passive resistance, which he termed *satyagraha*. He spoke of weaning your opponent '...from error by patience and compassion. For what appears to be truth to the one may appear to be error to the other. And patience means self-suffering. So the doctrine came to mean vindication of truth, not by infliction of suffering on the opponent, but on oneself.' Not, then, a strategy for the faint-hearted.

Having displayed willingness to risk physical harm and his liberty, Mandela took the next logical step of offering up his life for his cause. This is no more evident than in his conduct during the Rivonia Trial. There he outlined the ideals that he hoped to live to see achieved but for which he was prepared to die 'like a man'. That last phrase is telling, as it hints at the code of masculinity inherent in his tribal background that informed his conduct throughout his life. In *Long Walk to Freedom*, Mandela would explore the extent to which his and his co-defendants' lives were on a knife-edge during the episode. He explained how they had prepared themselves for the worse by accepting that it was a definite prospect to be faced up to rather than by holding out hope that they would ultimately be saved. To console himself, Mandela recalled a line from Shakespeare's *Measure for Measure*: 'Be absolute for death; for either death or life shall be the sweeter.'

While he did escape the death sentence, Mandela understood that he was now a marked man and he lived under that shadow for the rest of his life. Indeed, during the writing of this book, over twenty members of a white-supremacist militia group were convicted for a plot in the 2000s that included an assassination attempt on Mandela.

Given a life sentence at Rivonia, Mandela was forced to mine his reserves of courage still further during his twenty-seven years in prison. 'The cell is an ideal place to learn to know yourself, to search realistically and regularly the process of your own mind and feelings,' he wrote in a letter to Winnie in 1975. However, it was also a situation in which he might easily have succumbed to his demons. Somehow, though, the prison experience only strengthened his resolve to confront that which could have broken him.

In an interview he gave shortly after his release in

1990 he claimed that he could not remember losing his sense of control at any point, adding 'after all, in that situation you can only survive if you keep calm and cool'. It was this determination to survive that in part fuelled behaviour which to the onlooker might appear almost reckless. He took the prison authorities to task with regularity, staging protests, practising passive resistance by refusing to follow orders and even undertaking hunger strikes. All of this, as he well knew, made him a more likely target for the wrath of the system. But while some of us respond to intimidation by shrinking in to ourselves, it had the opposite effect on Mandela. As the prison system and the South African government conspired to rob him and his colleagues of their dignity, he became only more adamant that he would not buckle for, in his own words, 'I will not part with it at any price or under any pressure'.

Yet prison inevitably inflicted scars both mental and physical. Apart from the conscious brutalization, his health was badly affected by years spent in damp cells and his eyes suffered from the spells he spent working in a lime quarry without protective eyewear. The dust blocked up his tear ducts so that it is said he even lost the ability to cry. But throughout it all the will would not be crushed. As he wrote to Winnie from Robben Island:

Honour belongs to those who never forsake the truth even when things seem dark and grim, who try over and over again, who are never discouraged by insults, humiliations and even defeat.

Confronting the horrors of his prison-bound reality was thus another hill to be climbed on his long walk to freedom. In 1993 he explained to Richard Stengel that once you are free of the fear of your oppressor and the instruments of his oppression – for instance, prisons, the police and the army – you have disarmed him and are yourself liberated.

HOW DOES YOUR GARDEN GROW?

'A garden was one of the few things in prison that one could control. To plant a seed, watch it grow, to tend it and then harvest it, offered a simple but enduring satisfaction. The sense of being the custodian of this small patch of earth offered a taste of freedom.'

NELSON MANDELA, *LONG WALK TO FREEDOM*

There is a famous picture taken in 1977 of a rangy figure leaning on a spade by a small garden on Robben Island. It is called 'A Prisoner in the Garden' and its subject is Nelson Mandela. It was part of a mission by the South African authorities to persuade the world that conditions within the apartheid system were not as bleak as had been portrayed.

Whether they succeeded in that aim is doubtful

but the photo did capture the regime's most famous prisoner taking part in an activity that brought him great consolation. Mandela had some form when it came to gardening. He grew up in a rural area where he lived close to the land and had also worked on the professors' gardens at Fort Hare as part of a manual labour requirement, sparking his adult love of horticulture. Indeed, prior to his arrest and imprisonment in 1962, he is known to have evaded capture by disguising himself as a gardener.

However, it is one of those strange quirks of fate that the first garden he considered to be his own was the one he tended on Robben Island. It was a dusty vegetable patch that he was given permission to cultivate only after years of repeated requests. He took to the task with characteristic gusto, reading widely on the subject and adopting a trial-and-error approach to discern which crops to focus on, which fertilisers to use and so on. One of his guards even reported that – in the style of another famous horticulturalist, Prince Charles – he would talk to his plants. And all benefitted from his labours, from the inmates whose diets his produce enriched to the wardens who got to share some of the harvest too. Such opportunities to establish cordial ties with those who watched over him were rare and were not to be missed.

There was the odd difficult moment to contend

with, none more so than when the memoirs he had secretly been writing were discovered hidden in containers buried in the plot. But that gardening in general proved such a heartening distraction should come as no surprise. It allowed him to practise many of the qualities of leadership he could not, for the time being, exercise elsewhere. Gardening gave him responsibility for the welfare of living things. It allowed him to nurture them, required him to plan and experiment with strategies and approaches, called for patience, demanded he protect his charges from predators, and taught him when and how to save that which could be saved and sacrifice that which could not. Ultimately, too, he got to reap the rewards of his hard work and had the chance to call a small plot of land his own.

When he was transferred to Pollsmoor Prison in 1982, he found himself on good terms with its governor, who agreed to let him develop a rooftop garden. He loved his time there, away from the concrete sprawl of the rest of the site, spending as much as two hours a day tending his plants. It was a chance to be master in one aspect of life at least and brought him a small taste of freedom.

Gardening remained a passion in his post-prison life and in 1999, his wife, Graça, allowed the BBC programme *Ground Force* to secretly 'make-over' his garden in Qunu while the couple were away visiting President Bill Clinton. What Mandela made of it is not entirely clear but the show's producer described him as initially bemused before adding that he told his wife that they were not supposed to have any secrets. He surveyed the gardening team's handiwork with suitable good grace of course but for a man who gained so much in prison from having control over his garden, realising his plot at Qunu had been surrendered to the whim of strangers must have felt strange.

Embrace Culture

'Good art is invariably universal and timeless.'

NELSON MANDELA, 1980

M andela lived a full life in its truest sense. While many of history's great achievers have possessed a drive that manifests itself in tunnel vision, he sought to enjoy a broad range of experience. Behind the public façade was an individual intensely interested in the world about him and that included a fascination with the cultural landscape – both for its own sake and to increase his understanding of others.

He remained true to many of the cultural touchstones of his Xhosa heritage but was open to the traditions of others too – not least those who were ostensibly his enemies. Culture also had its role to play in his political life, helping to keep his name in the public domain while he was hidden away in prison and subsequently spreading his philosophy of forgiveness, egalitarianism and compassion.

'Something unique is the gift of longevity that God gave him and he used it to make big choices. When he was released after so much prosecution he could have chosen revenge but he chose redemption.'

JESSE JACKSON, 2013

Live a
Literary Life

'We can only achieve that better life for ordinary
people and citizens on our continent if we take
seriously and give priority to those simple precepts
of humanity that literature, good literature,
always deals with.'

NELSON MANDELA AT A BANQUET CELEBRATING
AFRICA'S HUNDRED BEST BOOKS OF THE
TWENTIETH CENTURY, 2002

Though Xhosa culture boasts a long oral tradition, a literary canon emerged from the nineteenth century onwards and the young Mandela lapped it up. His favourite Xhosa poet was S. E. K. Mqhayi, who was born in 1875 and died some seventy years later. Mqhayi was a historian too and his 1907 work, *U-Samson*, is widely regarded as the first novel in the Xhosa language. In addition, among his prolific output were several verses that would in due course be incorporated into multiracial South Africa's modern national anthem, 'Nkosi Sikelel' iAfrika' ('God Bless Africa'). In later life Mandela would describe Mqhayi as the 'poet laureate of the African people'.

Mandela also cultivated a deep childhood love for folktales, a great many of which were written down for the first time in the nineteenth and twentieth centuries. Following his retirement from public life, he put together a volume of *Favourite African Folktales*, bringing together thirty-two stories from across the continent and spanning the ages. In his foreword to the volume, he noted: 'This collection offers a handful of beloved stories, morsels rich with the gritty essence of Africa, but in many instances universal in their portrayal of humanity, beasts, and the mystical.' They, like Mandela himself, have a sort of dual existence, at once deeply rooted in a specific place and tradition while at the same time reflecting values and ideals common to us all.

Mandela, then, was a child immersed in the cultural heritage of his people. With his formal education came access to an even broader range of literature, into which he threw himself enthusiastically. In his old age he would reflect on the value of reading: 'When we read we are able to travel to many places, meet many people and understand the world. We can also learn how to deal with problems we are having by learning from the lessons of the past.'

So it was that he read writers from around the globe and from throughout the centuries. He gloried in the classics of ancient Greece (reading a Greek tragedy is 'one of the greatest experiences' he would tell his literary collaborator, Richard Stengel) as well as the great nineteenth-century English-language novelists and poets, developing a particular passion for Tennyson. He was an aficionado of Shakespeare too, along with Tolstoy and Steinbeck.

Nor did he restrict his reading to creations of the imagination. He read many of the foundation works of economics and educated himself in the writings of the giants of political theory, studying Marx, Lenin, Engels and Mao (all, of course, pivotal to his lifelong leaning towards socialism). There were also biographies of world figures like Churchill and John F. Kennedy, plus the great religious texts including the Bible and the Quran. It is a bibliography that screams of a man desperate to understand the motivations of his fellow humans.

As might be expected, he voraciously consumed books casting light on the nature of colonialism. He read Eddie Roux – a historian, botanist, founder member of the Young Communist League and member of the Communist Party of South Africa – whose most significant work was 1948's *Time Longer than Rope: A History of the Black Man's Struggle for Freedom in South Africa*. Also, Samir Amin's books on neo-colonialism, Amin being a Marxian economist of Egyptian origin. Then there was Roland Oliver and J.D. Fage's *Short History of Africa* – which when published in 1962 was one of the first authoritative single-volume histories of the continent – as well as H. A. L. Fisher's three-volume *A History of Europe*, published in 1935. Fisher, a President of the Board of Education in the British Liberal government of David Lloyd George from 1916–22, is perhaps as well known today as the man whose *post mortem* underwear was to play a vital role in the famed Operation Mincemeat counter-intelligence mission of the Second World War. A fate that no doubt offers a lesson of sorts on the fickle nature of fame!

Once the decision had been made by the ANC hierarchy to take up arms, a title of particular significance for Mandela was *The Revolt,* published in 1951 by Menachem Begin, the future premier of Israel. It tracks the activities of the author and those of the Irgun (also known as Etzel), the Zionist organization of which he was a part that waged war against British and Arab opposition in Palestine from the 1930s up until the establishment of the nation of Israel in 1948. Considered by many as a veritable handbook of guerrilla warfare, it held special interest for Mandela because Begin was operating in a land with little in the way of mountains and forests – territory similar to that of South Africa.

Inevitably, incarceration severely stifled Mandela's reading but could not snuff it out. Though access to literature was limited (more so at certain times), if desired texts were not readily to hand, efforts were made to have them smuggled in. On Robben Island there was an edition of the *Complete Works of Shakespeare* that a fellow inmate in the 1970s, Sonny Venkatrathnam, had persuaded the prison authorities to let him keep. Now known as the 'Robben Island Bible', it is signed by thirty-two prisoners, each of whom selected a passage that held particular resonance for them. Mandela put his name in it on 16 December 1977 against a line from *Julius Caesar*: 'Cowards die many times before their deaths.'

Before his imprisonment, he had read the *Diary of Anne Frank*, that tragic yet uplifting first-hand record of life as a Jew in hiding in the Nazi-occupied Netherlands. He read it again when a prisoner himself and found the experience entirely different now that he was able to identify with Anne's situation so much more closely. It also helped ferment his belief in direct action: '… the lessons of that tragedy sunk more deeply in our souls and also encouraged us in our situation because if a young girl of thirteen could take such militant action then we could follow the same example.'

He even turned his hand to a little light amateur dramatics while on Robben Island, appearing as Creon, King of Thebes in a production of Sophocles' *Antigone* – the mythological story of the daughter borne from the incestuous relationship between Jocasta and her own son, Oedipus. He evolved his passion for Greek tragedy in jail, describing them as 'enormously elevating'. 'What I took out of them,' he explained in *Long Walk to Freedom*, 'was that character was measured by facing up to difficult situations and that a hero was a man who would not break down even under the most trying circumstances.'

What he did not have access to was any of the literature from his own Xhosa culture. Though that wounded him, he partially filled the gap by reading several works in Afrikaans. One of his motivations for doing so was to try to better understand his captors, all of whom were Afrikaner. While his treatment at their hands was often cruel, he nonetheless saw the good in several of them and he considered that there was something to be gained by trying to better understand their cultural background.

One of the most important writers in Mandela's later life was Nadine Gordimer, who in 1991 was honoured with the Nobel Prize for Literature. The daughter of white immigrants, she is perhaps the foremost chronicler of apartheid South Africa and an active member of the

ANC. Her 1979 novel, *Burger's Daughter*, tells the story of a ring of white anti-apartheid activists attempting to overthrow the government and is credited with prompting Mandela to review his thoughts on traditional gender roles. Gordimer described the novel as a 'coded homage' to Bram Fischer, the Afrikaner lawyer who had defenced Mandela at his Rivonia trial. Mandela and Gordimer had already met before his imprisonment but in the years after his release, they developed a notable friendship.

In 1997, at the launch of *Madiba: The Rainbow Man* (a version of his life story aimed at children), Mandela spoke of the special pleasure he took in talking to children about reading, which he described as his favourite pastime. He was a man who spent long days and years immersed in words – to expand his understanding of the world, to gain an insight into his enemies' motivations and, finally, for the simple joy of reading itself.

INVICTUS

In the darkest times of his incarceration, Mandela was able to find succour in a copy of the poem 'Invictus' by the English poet William Henley which he is said to have kept on a scrap of paper. It is a poem that extols the strength of the human spirit even in the face of the grimmest adversity, so it is little surprise that Mandela connected so strongly with it. As he told Richard Stengel: 'When you read works of that nature you become encouraged. It puts life in you.'

'Invictus' first appeared in print in 1875. Though Henley was only in his mid-twenties at the time, he had suffered his fair share of hardship. Burdened by ill-health, he suffered a serious attack of tuber-culosis in his youth that caused one of his legs to be amputated. It is said that he wrote these verses to demonstrate his resilience despite this setback.

Initially untitled, the poem received the name 'Invictus' (Latin for 'unvanquished') from Sir Arthur Quiller-Couch when he included it in the *Oxford Book of English Verse* that he was editing. The poem ends with the powerful lines 'I am the master of my fate: I am the captain of my soul'.

Invictus also served as the title for a 2009 film directed by Clint Eastwood about South Africa's victory at their home Rugby Union World Cup in 1995 – an event that symbolised for many the arrival of post-apartheid South Africa on to the world stage (see page 180). In that movie, Mandela (played by Morgan Freeman) is shown inspiring the South African side's white captain, François Pienaar (played by Matt Damon), by giving him a copy of Henley's words. In real life, Mandela actually presented Pienaar with the 'Man in the Arena' section from Theodore Roosevelt's 1910 speech, 'Citizenship in a Republic'. Here, too, is that text, which carries a message Mandela holds dear:

It is not the critic who counts; not the man who points out how the strong man stumbles, or where the doer of deeds could have done them better. The credit belongs to the man who is actually in the arena, whose face is marred by dust and sweat and blood; who strives valiantly; who errs, who comes short again and again, because there is no effort without error and shortcoming; but who does actually strive to do the deeds; who knows great enthusiasms, the great devotions; who spends himself in a worthy cause; who at the best knows in the end the triumph of high achievement, and who at the worst, if he fails, at least fails while daring greatly, so that his place shall never be with those cold and timid souls who neither know victory nor defeat.

Play the Media

'He has wonderful inbuilt public relations
capabilities. He has a lot of charisma.'

F. W. DE KLERK, INTERVIEWED BY JOHN CARLIN
FOR PBS *FRONTLINE*, 1999

M andela's relationship with the media, especially the domestic media, was sometimes fraught and he was subjected to verbal assaults and invasions of privacy in common with many in the public eye. Nonetheless, he never wavered in his support of a free and robust media and acknowledged the role that newspapers in particular played in keeping him in touch with events in the world while he was jailed.

There was a time, though, when the press gunned for his very blood. As a youthful freedom-fighter, he found himself on the receiving end of overt hostility from the media establishment, particularly during the Rivonia Trial when certain newspapers and radio stations were actively calling for the defendants' hanging.

The relationship between Prisoner 46664 (the identification number Mandela was given when he was incarcerated) and the media then became rather more complicated. The authorities enforced a blanket ban on prisoners reading newspapers but he and his fellow inmates established a super-efficient newspaper smuggling enterprise. Perhaps because of their embargo, he subsequently valued access to print media highly, as when he told the Congress of the World Association of Newspapers in 2007: 'Not a day goes by when I don't read every newspaper I can lay my hands on, wherever I am.'

In *Long Walk to Freedom*, though, his attitude to the press may at best be described as ambivalent. Newspapers are, he argued, 'only a poor shadow of reality' and do not reveal great truths but are nonetheless useful for the way they show up the preconceptions and biases of both the journalists and editors working on them and those who read them. Yet on his release from jail, Mandela had praised the press for keeping alive the memory of the nation's political prisoners and spoke in terms of a sense of indebtedness to the media. He was equally effusive when addressing the 50th National Conference of the ANC in 1997:

> Instrumental in keeping us in touch and informed, in the dissemination of both the good news and the bad, the sensational and the mundane, has been the media. I wish to pay tribute on this occasion to their unflinching, and often ill-appreciated, commitment to their task and their contribution to a more informed and hence a better world.

That speech came a year after he had told the Cape Town Press Club that the media fraternity was not merely a critical observer of history but had an active role to play in the nation-building process then in full swing.

With justification, he did not always like the media but he knew that he needed them. For all those sections of the Fourth Estate that were antagonistic towards him, there were plenty more who played a crucial role in keeping him informed of events in the wider world while spreading his own message of equality and justice.

March to Your Own Beat

'Music is a great blessing. It has the power to
elevate and liberate us. It sets people free to
dream. It can unite us to sing with one voice.
Such is the value of music.'

NELSON MANDELA

If literature fundamentally impacted Mandela's life, music had a significant role to play too. He grew up on a diet of Xhosa folk songs and would come to describe African music as 'something that goes straight to your heart' and that 'tells the story of your own life, your living conditions, your aspirations.'

But just as his reading expanded and crossed cultures, so did his musical tastes. For instance, he fell in love with large parts of the canon of Western classical and choral music, developing a particular fondness for Tchaikovsky and Handel. He also adored the deep baritone of the African-American singer Paul Robeson, a man who away from the stage and recording studio sacrificed much in support of the burgeoning US civil rights movement.

While embracing the music of the West, Mandela kept a keen ear out for contemporary South African artists too. At their forefront was Miriam Makeba, an artist who was given the nickname 'Mama Africa' and of whom Mandela became a great fan after he moved to Johannesburg. She rose to stardom in the 1950s, introducing an international audience to hitherto unfamiliar traditional African melodies, often blended with other styles such as jazz. It was a fusion approach that other artists would take on in due course, perhaps most notably Paul Simon, whose 1986 album *Graceland* beautifully combined African rhythms with American popular music.

While its production upset many who believed it flaunted the cultural boycott then in place, Makeba, a noted anti-apartheid campaigner, was not among them as she agreed to appear with Simon during his 1987 *Graceland* tour. Exiled from her homeland in 1963 for her activism, she returned to South Africa in 1990 at the personal request of the recently freed Mandela. A few years later, he was quoted as saying: 'Few South Africans have not been moved by Miriam Makeba's haunting melodies that have given voice to the pain of exile and dislocation, at the same time inspiring a powerful sense of hope.'

Another black South African artist who found favour with him was Hugh Masekela, a respected musician and vocalist whose song 'Bring Him Back Home' became something of an anti-apartheid anthem. Music was vital in maintaining morale among Mandela and his fellow inmates and Mandela was a regular participant in Christmas concerts in prison. He and his fellow inmates also sang folksongs as they worked, not only for the comfort they provided but as a medium of defiance. As Mandela saw it, the prison authorities were intent on breaking their spirits but the singing of what he called 'freedom songs' bolstered the prisoners' determination to hold strong. Furthermore, many of the songs had subversive lyrics that often went over the heads of the guards. Not all their song choices were edgy though. It is a curiosity that one of the songs Mandela sang behind bars was the old, sentimental Scottish ballad, 'Bonny Mary of Argyle'.

While most of us have a relationship with music that extends only to listening or playing, Mandela had the distinction of having personally inspired a significant canon of works, taking in an array of musical styles. In the 1980s the Special AKA's 'Free Nelson Mandela' became a protest song *extraordinaire*, while for fans of stadium rock, there was the track '46664 (Long Walk to Freedom)', written by the Clash's Joe Strummer and U2's Bono. Those of a classical bent, meanwhile, might prefer Wilhelm Kaizer Lendemann's 'Homage a Nelson M. for cello and percussion, Op 27'. Then there was 'My Black President' by the South African pop singer Brenda Fassie, a song banned on its release in 1989 but joyfully played at Mandela's inauguration ceremony in 1994. A 'Nelson Mandela's Greatest Hits' compilation would fill a vast playlist.

PACK EARPLUGS

Not only did Mandela inspire music in others, he was also the driving force behind a number of concerts that garnered worldwide attention. The 46664 concerts series has included shows since 2003 in locations as diverse as the South African cities of Johannesburg, Cape Town and George, along with Madrid (Spain), Tromsø (Norway) and London (UK). Their aim was to raise awareness of HIV/AIDS, though the last doubled as a ninetieth birthday tribute to Mandela.

Then there were the two landmark concerts held at the UK's Wembley Stadium in 1988 and 1990. The first, dubbed the Nelson Mandela Seventieth Birthday Tribute Concert, took place on 11 June 1988 and attracted an estimated global audience of 600 million people. Three years earlier, the Live Aid concert at the same venue had shown how such an event could focus attention on a particular cause (in that case, famine in Ethiopia). The Mandela concert, though, was a more politicised affair as artists sought to keep his plight in the public eye as he faced his twenty-fifth year in prison.

Before the concert, twenty-four Conservative Members of the UK Parliament put down a House of Commons motion criticising the BBC for giving 'publicity to a movement that encourages the African National Congress in its terrorist activities'. The concert was a triumph nonetheless, introducing Mandela's fight to a new generation via a stellar list of performers including Sting, Tracy Chapman, Al Green, The Bee Gees, Stevie Wonder, Youssou N'Dour, Whitney Houston, Eric Clapton and Jessye Norman.

On 16 April 1990, Wembley hosted Nelson Mandela: An International Tribute for a Free South Africa. Again, there was a fabulous roll-call of performers but the atmosphere was altogether more triumphant as Mandela had walked out of Victor Verster Prison a free man the previous month. If perhaps not all of the music was to Mandela's personal taste, he was a man who surely knew better than anyone just how powerful music can be.

Be Adaptable

'If you wait for textbook conditions,
they will never occur.'

NELSON MANDELA, *LONG WALK TO FREEDOM*

As a student of rebellion and military and guerrilla strategy, Mandela learned that the ability to adapt to particular circumstances could be the difference between victory and defeat. It was a point he made strongly in the 'No Easy Walk to Freedom' speech he made to his ANC colleagues in 1953, when he emphasized how important it was for any political movement to keep in touch with reality and with the prevailing conditions within which it was working.

His personal skills for adaptation were amply in evidence as he went underground in 1961 to evade capture by the authorities. It was during this period that he earned the nickname of the 'Black Pimpernel' – an arch reference to Sir Percy Blakeney, eponymous hero of Baroness Orczy's 1905 work, *The Scarlet Pimpernel.* In that tale, the aristocratic Blakeney uses his wits and aptitude for disguise to repeatedly escape the guillotine during the French Revolution. During his own time on the run, Mandela variously masqueraded as a student, a farm labourer, an agricultural demonstrator, a nightwatchman, a petrol attendant and a chauffeur. When he was finally arrested in 1962, he was at the time passing himself off as one David Motsamayi.

Flexibility and initiative were watchwords throughout his career, whether he was orchestrating protests and formulating strategy while avoiding the reach of the authorities or simply fighting for his survival once he had been ensnared by the prison system. Indeed, the demands of incarceration called on all those who refused to be submerged by it to increases their resourcefulness. For instance, prisoners on Robben Island developed a highly sophisticated smuggling operation to get news and intelligence into and away from their cells. According to Mandela: 'Not even the most repressive regime can stop human beings from finding ways of communicating and obtaining access to information.'

He rapidly grasped that in order to overcome the challenges faced on a daily basis – from coping with solitary confinement to enduring the rigours of physical labour and finding ways to stay mentally alert – prisoners had no choice but to adjust if they were not to break. Nevertheless, he never became blasé about the ability of people to cope in the most testing of environments. In a letter he sent to Adelaide, Oliver Tambo's wife, in 1970, he specifically discussed his amazement at the ability of the human soul and human body to adapt and toughen to cope with hardship.

Part of his own coping process involved attempting to turn disadvantage to advantage wherever possible. Sometimes it wasn't achievable but Mandela became a master of finding a way of extracting something good from something bad. Most fundamentally, as we have already seen, he used his time in incarceration to develop his mental toughness and explore new approaches to fighting the apartheid system. This resilience is neatly captured in a Justice Department report of 1981 – some nineteen years after he had entered prison – which found that the experience had neither had a detrimental effect on his idealism or on his self-belief. There can hardly have been a bigger slap in the face for the authorities.

His refusal to bow under the pressures of jail life was a regular theme in his correspondence with Winnie. In a letter from 1970, for instance, he told her he was convinced that 'floods of personal disaster can never drown a determined revolutionary'. Five years later and he was discussing how some men could be broken by the difficulties they face while others were made by them – and he clearly counted himself in the latter group.

In 1985 the Commonwealth established an 'Eminent Persons Group' to investigate and report on apartheid in South Africa. When they spoke to Mandela, he told them: 'There is nothing like a long spell in prison to focus your mind, and to bring you to a more sober appreciation of the realities of your society.' Certainly, Mandela and many of his colleagues turned their prison wings into crucibles of intellectual and ideological dynamism. It is something of an irony that Robben Island could claim to be the ANC's premier think-tank. Mandela also took the opportunity to meditate, a process he believed yielded rich rewards even as it forced him to confront negative aspects of his life. As he would tell Winnie: 'Never forget that a saint is a sinner who keeps on trying.'

Crucially, he also accepted that he and others would fall to errors of judgement and make the odd mis-step along the way. He wrote in his unpublished autobiography of the mid-1970s:

> Only armchair politicians are immune from committing mistakes. Errors are inherent in political action. Those who are in the centre of political struggle, who have to deal with practical and pressing problems, are afforded little time for reflection and no precedents to guide them and are bound to slip up many times.

But as he was prepared to forgive others, so he was also prepared to forgive himself. A refusal to do so would surely have shattered the spirit of someone already living in such an oppressive atmosphere. It is suggestive of the enduring streak of optimism that just maybe saved his health and sanity over a lifetime of trials and tribulations. His belief in finding the positive where negatives seemingly reign was never better expressed than to his daughter, Zindzi, in 1979: 'There are few misfortunes in this world that you cannot turn into a personal triumph if you have the iron will and the necessary skill.'

Be the Bigger Person

'We must use time wisely and forever realize
that the time is always ripe to do right.'

NELSON MANDELA

M andela's moral authority partially rested on his ability to emerge from points of conflict and tension as, more often than not, the bigger, more gracious and morally justified of the parties involved. He put himself in the way of danger in the interests of others and, even when engaged in armed struggle, sought to avoid harm to civilians. He then stepped back from violence when it had achieved its aims of bringing the government to the negotiating table. Nor did he take the opportunities available during his presidency and celebrated retirement to settle old scores or shame those who used to target him. Essential to his aura of moral rectitude was his facility for forgiveness rather than vengeance.

Forced first to live as an outlaw and then survive as a prisoner, Mandela had innumerable sufferings – some obvious and others less tangible but no less damaging – inflicted upon him. That he did not succumb whole-heartedly to bitterness is a remarkable achievement that should not be overlooked. As Bill Clinton put it: 'Thank God that the person who occupied the cell was able to live all those years in that way without having his heart turned to stone, without giving up on his dream for South Africa.'

Instead, Mandela's presidency was marked by several epic gestures of reconciliation. The donning of the Springbok rugby shirt in 1995 (see page 181) springs to mind but equally impressive was his decision to take tea with Betsie Verwoerd. She was the widow of H. F. Verwoerd, South Africa's Prime Minister from 1958 until his assassination in 1966 and one of the chief architects of the apartheid project. It was during Verwoerd's tenure that Mandela and his fellow ANC leaders received their life sentences at the Rivonia Trial. He met his former nemesis' widow in 1995 at her home in Orania, a privately-owned town in the Northern Cape established in 1990 as an Afrikaner-only enclave.

The meeting was cordial though he did manage a single cheeky sideswipe at his one-time oppressor when he commented on the town's statue of H. F. Verwoerd (measuring just under six feet): 'Well, you made him very small.' It was a comment indicative of a man who has long found refuge in humour, even though the Xhosa culture he grew up in looked down on laughter among its leaders. Mandela, though, reached the conclusion that laughter and seriousness need not be mutually exclusive. In fact, he believes humour to be a useful strategic weapon in the search for common ground. In a 2005 interview for *Mandela: The Authorised Portrait* he said:

I like, you know, people being relaxed because even when you are discussing a serious matter, relaxation is very important because it encourages your thinking; so I like to make jokes even when examining serious situations. Because when people are relaxed they can think properly.

Though many wondered at his decision to make the trip to Orania, he described his reception as comparable to that which he might expect in Soweto. The entire enterprise made a powerful statement that South Africa was indeed changing and that the process would happen more quickly by the breaking of bread between enemies rather than by extracting revenge for past wrongs. His willingness to consign the past to history – from where its lessons may be learned dispassionately – was evidenced again with news of Betsie's death in 2000 when she was ninety-eight. He commended her for her 'pure Afrikaner hospitality' and said of Betsie and her husband that they were part of the nation's history even though he condemned their policies.

The 1995 Rugby Union World Cup Final (where Mandela wore the Springbok shirt) and the Verwoerd meeting were just two instances among many that show Mandela's willingness not only to eschew vengeance but to treat his long-standing opponents generously. It was a tactic he explained in *Long Walk to Freedom*: 'If you want to make peace with an enemy, one must work with that enemy and that enemy becomes your partner.'

While he did not simply offer a clean slate, once the channels of communication had been opened up he focussed less on differences between the sides and more on commonalities.

He once explained how even as a boy, he would seek to overcome his rivals without humiliating them since humiliation was in his opinion an unnecessarily cruel fate. His preference for cordial engagement over open conflict was there in his prison days too, when he decided to learn Afrikaans in the hope of better communicating with his jailers. As he explained in an essay he wrote in 1976:

> We ought to speak directly to the Afrikaner and fully explain our position. Honest men are to be found on both sides of the colour line and the Afrikaner is no exception...

Nor was his willingness to engage with the opposition ever a sign of weakness. His talks with the government, for instance, happened only after establishing ground rules. When he risked the wrath of his ANC colleagues to make secret contact with the government of P. W. Botha in the mid-1980s, he turned down the proffered carrot of his own freedom. Instead, he insisted that the ANC would not lay down arms until they had gained political power; demanded recognition for the Communist Party and insisted that the government accept the principle of majority rule.

While walking a tightrope between ANC mistrust and the State's attempts to isolate him, he succeeded in building a bond of mutual respect with first Botha and then his successor, F. W. de Klerk. Both Prime Ministers would note the politeness he always brought to talks and both were wowed by his knowledge of the historical Afrikaner resistance movement. (It was, of course, one of the grand ironies of the apartheid years that the Afrikaner oppressors had considered themselves an oppressed minority within South Africa just a few decades earlier.)

In the end, Mandela's willingness to put aside personal grievances and to turn the other cheek was a deeply pragmatic tactic within a much larger game. It is a philosophy he enlarged upon in an interview with the *Christian Science Monitor* in 2000:

If you have an objective in life, then you want to concentrate on that and not engage in infighting with your enemies. You want to create an atmosphere where you can move everybody towards the goal you have set for yourself – as well as the collective for which you work.

THE TRUTH AND RECONCILIATION COMMISSION

Mandela was never so naïve as to believe that the injustices perpetrated on all sides in the apartheid era could be swept under the carpet. In 1994, he told the annual conference of the South African Methodist Church: 'We have to forgive the past but, at the same time, ensure that the dignity of the victims is restored, and their plight properly addressed.'

The single greatest instrument in the pursuit of this goal was the Truth and Reconciliation Commission (TRC). Established by statute in 1995, it began operating the following year under the stewardship of Archbishop Desmond Tutu. The overall aim was to bear witness to and record the wrongs of the past so that the country could move into the future with a clear conscience. It was based in part on a similar body set up in Chile, which had reported in 1991 on politically-motivated deaths and disappearances during the rule of Augusto Pinochet in the 1970s and 1980s.

The TRC could not grant victims any formal judicial or financial restitution but offered possible amnesty for those who confessed to committing politically-motivated crimes and misdeeds between 1960 and 1994. Though based in Cape

Town, hearings were held throughout the country, with work divided between three committees:

- ⊙ The Human Rights Violations Committee, to establish breaches of human rights.
- ⊙ The Reparation and Rehabilitation Committee, designed to restore victims' dignity and help with rehabilitation.
- ⊙ The Amnesty Committee, which considered the cases of individuals applying for amnesty.

Given the sensitivity of the events under review, it was inevitable that not everyone would be a fan of the TRC. One of the major complaints against it was that it let perpetrators of unspeakable crimes get off too lightly. Should a murderer, for instance, be spared a formal criminal trial just because he killed in the name of the government? The family of Steve Biko – the thirty-one-year-old founder of the Black Consciousness Movement who died in police custody in 1977 – notably described the TRC as a 'vehicle for political expediency' that 'robbed' them of their fundamental right to justice.

On occasion, it could seem toothless as well. P.W. Botha, for instance, simply refused to appear despite having been issued with a subpoena. He called the process a 'circus' and even had the fine and suspended sentence imposed on him for non-attendance overturned on appeal. However, in general the TRC could not be accused of being a light touch, since only some 850 amnesty requests were granted from some 7,000 applications. The ANC itself came in for harsh criticism and some figures in the party were keen to suppress publication of the Commission's findings in 1998, though Mandela argued strongly against such a course of action.

In due course, similar bodies were set up in countries across South America, Europe, Africa and Asia where dictatorships or civil wars had riven communities. While not perfect, the TRC was a vital stage in South Africa's healing process. In 1996, Mandela described it thus:

Ordinary South Africans are determined that the past be known, the better to ensure that it is not repeated. They seek this, not out of vengeance, but so that we can move into the future together. The choice of our nation is not whether the past should be revealed, but rather to ensure that it comes to be known in a way which promotes reconciliation and peace.

Keep a Part of Yourself Private

'From experience I have found that a family photo
is everything in prison and you must have it
right from the beginning.'

NELSON MANDELA, 1969

As a figure of global importance, Mandela endured a quite extraordinary level of personal scrutiny. It is little surprise, then, that he jealously guarded his right to a private life. As he wrote in a letter to Winnie, his second wife, in 1975: 'There are affairs in life where third parties, no matter who they are, should not be let in at all.'

However, he fought a losing battle on this front at least, and increasingly so in his declining years. As he lay in hospital in 2013, his health in tatters, there were unseemly episodes of family feuding played out in the public eye. Having married three times and had six children, seventeen grandchildren and fourteen great-grandchildren, Mandela was the patriarch of a family empire with many competing interests. With the end of his life approaching, the battle to be in pole position to benefit from his legacy, image and – let's not beat about the bush – his enduring bankability saw the family turn in on itself, with several internecine lawsuits actioned at the time of writing.

If Mandela's conduct in public life was guided by remarkable vision and great instincts, by his own admission his private life was far murkier. As he wrote in

Long Walk to Freedom:'My commitment to my people, to the millions of South Africans I would never know or meet, was at the expense of the people I knew best and loved most.'

In an interview published in the *Daily Mail* newspaper in 2010, his daughter Maki (offspring from his first marriage) came to much the same conclusion. She was quoted as saying:

> I still think that after he was released, he should have created some space for the family, for his children. We were ignored, or at least not acknowledged, while he was preoccupied with politics... I really do think he could have done things a little bit differently. Even now, when he's got more time, he doesn't make the effort to really engage. He's open and extrovert to the world, but awkward in his intimate personal relationships with his own family.

It is a portrayal backed up by a passage in the 1997 book, *Every Secret Thing: My Family, My Country*, by Gillian Slovo (daughter of Joe). She described how Mandela had once told her of an incident when he tried to embrace his grown-up daughter only to have his advance rejected with the words,'You are the father to all our people, but you never had the time to be a father to me.'

The imponderable question is whether it would have been possible for him to be a committed family man and still achieve what he did in the public sphere. The strong suspicion is that the balancing of private and public lives was almost certainly unachievable. Perhaps Mandela's greatest mistake was to ever think otherwise.

On the other hand, such was the importance of family to him that it is difficult to imagine that he would have had the strength and energy to lead the anti-apartheid movement without it. In a 1979 letter to Winnie he described family life as 'an important pillar to any public man'. He had previously told her that 'physical suffering is nothing' when set against the fraying of matrimonial and familial bonds. It was a theme he revisited on his return to Robben Island as a visitor in 1994, when he spoke of how he had been 'terribly lonesome for my wife and my family' as a convict there.

Clearly, there was a contradiction between the man hungry for a private life and the one who would sacrifice virtually anything for his public duty (though as Mandela noted in a letter of 1987: 'Contradictions are an essential part of life and never cease tearing one apart.'). He has spoken of the difficulty in watching his children grow up virtually devoid of his own influence and guidance and then, when he was free again, having his time consumed by the needs of the nation. There must be a deep irony for Mandela's offspring that he is very possibly regarded more as a father figure by the nation at large than by they themselves. The conflict between duty to your family and to your people was one Mandela never happily resolved, as he explained in *Long Walk to Freedom*:

I wondered – not for the first time – whether one was ever justified in neglecting the welfare of one's own family in order to fight for the welfare of others. Can there be anything more important than looking after one's aging mother? Is politics merely a pretext for shirking one's responsibilities, an excuse for not being able to provide in the way one wanted?

When Mandela retired, he returned to Qunu, the village of his childhood. It may be assumed with some confidence that he hoped to find some solace there, away from the public gaze but within the bosom of his family. That his final days saw the very public airing of much dirty laundry is the somewhat sad proof that he achieved more as a nation-builder than a home-maker.

MANDELA'S WIVES

EVELYN

Mandela's first marriage, in 1944, was to Evelyn Mase. It lasted fourteen years and produced four children but had run its course some time before it was formally dissolved.

Evelyn was born in Engcobo in the Transkei. After she was orphaned at twelve, she was sent to Soweto to be under the care of her brother. He was a political activist and had grown close to his cousin, Walter Sisulu. Evelyn became friendly with Albertina, the future Mrs Sisulu, and it was through the Sisulus that Evelyn was introduced to Mandela in the early 1940s.

Their first years of marriage were by all accounts happy but Mandela was increasingly active in the ANC as well as trying to establish his legal practice after many years of study. Evelyn had little interest in politics but did provide a steady family base for him. However, in 1954 she became a Jehovah's Witness, a move not popular with her husband. They sparred over religion and politics and she offered him an ultimatum: her or the ANC. She lost his vote. As he would later recall:

When I would tell her that I was serving the nation, she would reply that serving God was above serving the nation. A man and woman who hold such different views of their respective roles in life cannot remain close.

Evelyn moved out with the children and they divorced in 1958 amid accusations of adultery against Mandela that would come to public light in Fatima Meer's 1988 unauthorised biography, *Higher than Hope*. Evelyn also accused him of being violent towards her, though he always denied this, bar one exchange where he said he defended himself when she came at him with a poker.

Wherever the truth lies, it was a sad end to their particular episode of love's young dream.

In 1998, Evelyn remarried. Her second husband was a Jehovah's Witness and a retired businessman from Soweto, Simon Rakeepile. She died on 30 April 2004.

WINNIE

Mandela's second wife, Winnie spent the majority of her married life with her husband in prison. Carrying on the anti-apartheid fight on his behalf, she became a controversial and divisive figure within South African society.

Winnie Madikizela was born in the village of Mbongweni in the Transkei on 26 September 1936 and qualified as a social worker, taking up a job in Johannesburg. Pretty, sparkling and a paid-up member of the ANC, she came to the attention of Mandela and they married in June 1958, shortly after his divorce from Evelyn was granted. Winnie bore him two children before he was arrested in 1962 and his long years of incarceration began.

In his absence, she did much to keep the flame of their struggle alive. She was, in turn, subjected to mistreatment by the police and was served with a succession of banning orders that severely curtailed her freedoms. Mandela, meanwhile, felt guilt as a result of his enforced abandonment of her and for the fact that she was persecuted on account of their association. He was, undoubtedly, passionately in love with her.

However, Winnie was far from a helpless victim and adopted increasingly violent tactics in the fight against apartheid. In 1986, for instance, she made a notorious speech in which she endorsed 'necklacing' – a particularly gruesome punishment against suspected collaborators that involved hanging burning tyres round the neck of the victim, often resulting in death. In 1988, members of her personal bodyguard, the so-called Mandela United Football Club (MUFC), were implicated in the death of a black child, Stompie Seipei, whom they suspected of being an informer. Winnie was by then considered a loose cannon within the anti-apartheid movement and Mandela found himself in a difficult position as he avoided publicly condemning her conduct.

When he was released in 1990, Winnie was there to meet him and stood proudly by his side but their marriage was on borrowed time. In 1991 she was convicted of kidnap and accessory to assault in relation to the Stompie Seipei incident. And while her husband was calling for calm and patience as talks went on with the government, she adopted a harder line. The couple split in 1992 though Mandela made a statement claiming he retained the same love and affection for her that he had on first meeting her and kept while in prison. She was appointed Deputy Minister of Arts, Culture, Science and Technology in his government in 1994 but was gone within a year amid corruption allegations. In 1996, she and Mandela divorced.

The Truth and Reconciliation Commission, reporting in 1998, found Winnie 'politically and morally accountable for the gross violations of human rights committed by the MUFC' and concluded that she had been directly and indirectly responsible for murders, torture, abductions and assaults against men, women and children.

Further convictions for fraud occurred in the early 2000s. But still she commands fervent support from some in South Africa, while attracting the opprobrium of others. She is most certainly an enigmatic figure whose influence on Mandela was vast. But when the time came for him to turn from freedom-fighter to statesman, their paths diverged.

GRAÇA
Mandela's third wife after marrying him on his 80th birthday in 1998, Graça Machel is a renowned humanitarian, particularly on women's and children's issues. She is the only woman to have been First Lady in two different nations.

She was born Graça Simbine on 17 October 1945 in the Gaza Province of what was then Portuguese East Africa and which would become Mozambique. Having studied in Portugal, she became a teacher back in the country of her birth and an activist within its independence movement. When Mozambique won independence in 1975, she served as Minister of Education and Culture in its first government led by Samora Machel. She married President Machel in September that year, only to be widowed in 1986 when his presidential plane crashed on its way home from a summit in Zambia.

Her work in the field of human rights has won her many admirers and she has undertaken projects for various international organizations including the UN, UNESCO and UNICEF. She was also the recipient of numerous awards and honours, including a Damehood from the British government. Her profile only increased on marrying Mandela in 1998 and she was key to the establishment of the Elders (see page 198), of which she remains a member.

Master the Art of Negotiation

'No problem is so deep that it cannot be overcome, given the will of all parties, through discussion and negotiation rather than force and violence.'

NELSON MANDELA, PRESIDENT'S
BUDGET DEBATE, 1999

As head of the ANC and its many disparate wings, as a prisoner attempting to engage the government in talks, as a free man plotting his country's future direction and as President of that country, Mandela spent his life negotiating with marked success.

For him, negotiation and compromise went hand in hand, on the grounds that the former is pointless if you are not prepared to do the latter. It is a culture he was exposed to from his earliest days, when he and his friends would gather to watch the Thembu community elders discuss the collective way forward based on the wealth of their individual wisdom and experience. It was a model of negotiation that he clung to, with everyone having the choice to offer an opinion and the option to accept or reject the opinions of others. In 2010 he was quoted in the documentary *Viva Madiba*: 'We have been brought up in the tradition of collective leadership. We discuss matters thoroughly, differ sometimes very sharply but eventually we reach a consensus.'

Of course, negotiating in an environment where everyone is ultimately pulling in the same direction is vastly different from negotiating with an entrenched opponent pursuing an entirely different agenda. That, though, was Mandela's challenge in dealing with the apartheid regime, especially from the 1980s onwards. They were difficult years in which a step forward could easily be followed by three back.

At times, the government – operating from its position of power – was unbearably stubborn. At other moments, it was his own side that exhorted him to hold to particular lines so that in the end he felt compelled to initiate some talks in secret. Then there were the temptations to rise above – repeatedly he resisted promises of freedom until he had extracted concession that would benefit the wider movement.

Even after 1990, when de Klerk's government seemed more willing to bend, Mandela had to call upon all of his well-honed negotiating skills. In general, he believed in slow deliberation before making a move but on occasion he needed to make snap decisions and trust his instincts. Some of his own support interpreted this as a tendency towards authoritarianism that hardly seems justified in retrospect, even if he did prize control in any given situation.

Talks with the government were further muddied by escalating violence in the country but by 1991 a national peace accord was in place. The murder of Communist Party leader Chris Hani in 1993 by a right-winger was another flashpoint that threatened civil war. It fell to Mandela to plead for peace, something he did with such aplomb that it convinced many of his presidential credentials. It is not to overstate the case that he was negotiating for the very future of the country when he addressed the nation on television:

> Tonight I am reaching out to every single South African, black and white, from the very depths of my being. A white man, full of prejudice and hate, came to our country and committed a deed so foul that our whole nation now teeters on the brink of disaster. A white woman, of Afrikaner origin, risked her life so that we may know, and bring to justice, this assassin. The cold-blooded murder of Chris Hani has sent shock waves throughout the country and the world. ... Now is the time for all South Africans to stand together against those who, from any quarter, wish to destroy what Chris Hani gave his life for – the freedom of all of us.

Having played his part in pulling the country back from the brink, Mandela returned to the negotiating table opposite the government. Within a year he was triumphing at the country's first multiracial elections. Throughout, he realized that this could only be achieved by making concessions along the way and providing reassurance to the white population who were understandably nervous of what the future might hold. He was magnanimous, admitting that over the course of the struggle no side could claim to be absolutely in the right and the other side in the wrong. 'Compromise means each of the parties involved should give away something to the other, should accommodate the demands, the fears, of the other party,' he said in an interview with the South African Broadcasting Corporation in 1990.

So how might Mandela's attitude to negotiation be best summed up? Perhaps by remembering the words he spoke in an interview with the BBC in 1993: 'The most powerful weapon is not violence but it is talking to people.'

'He is not a manipulator. He is not a man who speaks with different tongues to different people.'

GEORGE BIZOS, INTERVIEWED BY JOHN CARLIN
FOR PBS *FRONTLINE*, 1999

Lessons in
Birthing a Nation

'The freedoms which democracy brings will remain
empty shells if they are not accompanied by real
and tangible improvements in the material lives
of millions of ordinary citizens...'

NELSON MANDELA IN *VIVA MADIBA:*
A HERO FOR ALL SEASONS, 2010

On 10 May 1994 Mandela was sworn in as President of the Rainbow Nation, just over four years after he was released from prison. It had been a difficult journey since he had stepped out of Victor Verster Prison. Not only had he needed to reach agreement with the National Party government and overcome resistance from parts of the white population but he also saw the ANC virtually at war with Chief Buthelezi's Inkatha Freedom Party, an organization that had once stood shoulder to shoulder with Mandela in the fight against apartheid. Now he was seventy-five years old and his life's ambition of bringing multiracial democracy to South Africa was complete. Yet, it can easily be argued that the hard work was only just about to begin.

If good governance is about striking a balance between sound ideology and practical considerations, it was a subject Mandela touched upon in a notebook dating from 1962. Then his concern was not national government but governance of the ANC and the wider anti-apartheid movement: 'Whilst political consciousness is vital to the formation of an army and in mobilising mass support, practical matters must not be lost sight of.'

Back to the 1990s, and once the de Klerk government had promised free and fair elections, Mandela set his mind to the practical problems a democratically-elected government might face. Which was also to say, the challenges he might face as a frontrunner for the presidency. Between 1992 and 1994 there is a distinct shift in his public declarations away from broad democratic ideals towards far more pragmatic concerns. Consider his statement in 1992 that 'without democracy there cannot be peace', his pre-election highlighting of the inadequacy of 'freedom without bread' and 'bread without freedom', and the following from 1994: 'Freedom is meaningless if people cannot put food in their stomachs, if they can have no shelter, if illiteracy and disease continue to dog them.'

He long espoused that social equality is the only basis for human happiness and described poverty as a 'terrible thing'. However, his goal of improving the material lot of the black majority proved an elusive one. At the launch of the 'Make Poverty History' project in London in 2005, he described poverty as something not natural but man-made and therefore eradicable by human actions. That, as he knew well by then, is much easier said than done.

Confronted with housing shortages and rampant unemployment, Mandela as president was forced to move away from his instinctive leaning towards socialism – particularly in light of the then recent collapse of communism in Europe – and to embrace the International Monetary Fund and its liberal capitalist agenda. Still, though, progress on the ground was and continues to be slow, as the 2011 census results show. With 79 per cent of the population classified as black, income inequality remains rife, with the average income of a white household coming in at 365,000 rand (about US$42,000) and that of a black household measuring 60,600 rand (about US$7,000). Meanwhile, according to the World Bank, those living below the national poverty line increased from 31 per cent to 38 per cent between 1995 and 2000 before falling back to 23 per cent in 2006. Hardly evidence of a brave new world.

If his domestic policies met with limited success, Mandela nonetheless remained a giant on the international scene as he built his foreign policy around the human rights agenda. He was central to the peace processes in Angola and the Congo region, and though there were failures too – such as his unsuccessful intervention to save the life of Nigerian environmental activist Ken Saro-Wiwa – in broad terms, Mandela ended his tenure an even larger figure internationally than when he took office.

Was Mandela's presidency a success, then? It is perhaps still too early to say for sure. His overriding achievement was to keep the country together so that two decades after his election, multiracial democracy is now well established and the country has not descended into civil strife.

However, there were significant deficiencies. The

AIDS crisis was not addressed – including some of the unhelpful attitudes to sex and sexuality ingrained in a still patriarchal society that values traditional notions of masculinity. For Mandela, it was perhaps just a fight too far for the burgeoning nation to contend with. He did, of course, seek to make amends in his retirement but it is a scourge with which this and future generations must grapple from a position of weakness.

Nor did the Mandela administration get to grips with the poverty endemic among the black population, which in turn fed into an epidemic of violent crime. This was surely the greatest shortcoming. Mandela, then, built a nation whose democratic institutions have so far proved robust and brought South Africa out of its decades of international isolation. To this extent, he achieved his aims and should be considered a success. He did not, though, rebalance the economic inequalities that continue to impact the country. It was, maybe, simply too great a job to be done in the available timeframe. Whatever the reasons, it was a goal he had set his mind to but which he failed to reach. Proof that even the greatest figures cannot work miracles.

GOING OFFLINE

On assuming office, Mandela was wary of the excesses and inequalities inherent in Western capitalism, while world communism was mired in crisis. Given these circumstances, he signed South Africa up to the Non-Aligned Movement, a semi-formal grouping of countries that do not identify with any particular power bloc. It was a move indicative of his desire to plough his own furrow on the global scene.

This attitude was controversially expressed in the cordial relations he pursued with figures widely seen as international pariahs. So, for instance, he had a good relationship with Libya's Colonel Gaddafi, a fellow revolutionary who offered moral support to the anti-apartheid movement (Mandela was the first recipient of the Al-Gaddafi International Prize for Human Rights in 1989). However, by the 1980s Gaddafi had garnered an unenviable reputation for domestic authoritarianism and state-sponsored terrorism. Mandela, though, opposed UN sanctions against Libya and helped negotiate the terms of the troubled trial of a Libyan national accused of the 1986 Lockerbie terrorist bombing. While Gaddafi and Mandela had their moments of disagreement, the South African statesman was a rare ally to his North African counterpart.

Mandela also refused to turn his back on a profound friendship he had built up with the head of communist Cuba, Fidel Castro. A socialist, anti-imperialist hero to some and a human rights-abusing dictator to others, Castro was one of Mandela's most fervent supporters during his years of rebellion. Castro's own triumph in the Cuban Revolution in 1959 had been an inspiration to the youthful Mandela, who also believed that Cuba's military support (numbering perhaps as many as 300,000 troops) in the Angolan civil war in the 1970s and 1980s had been crucial in destabilising the South African government then embroiled in the conflict. Such was the impact, Mandela believed, that Cuba had played a vital part in giving the anti-apartheid movement a real chance of prevailing.

After his release, Mandela was quick to credit his old comrade, thanking Cuba for the financial, military and medical resources it had provided. On a visit to the country in 1991, Mandela said: 'The Cuban people hold a special place in the hearts of the people of Africa. The Cuban internationalists have made a contribution to African independence, freedom, and justice, unparalleled for its principled and selfless character.'

Castro was typically effusive in returning the compliment:

If one wanted an example of an absolutely upright man, that man, that example, would be Mandela. If one wanted an example of an unshakably firm, courageous, heroic, calm, intelligent, and capable man, that example and that man would be Mandela. I did not just reach this conclusion after having met him in person... I have thought this for many years. I identify him as one of the most extraordinary symbols of this era.

Mandela might have kept some dangerous company that did not go down well with Washington or the governments of Western Europe, but he was a man of honour when it came to remembering who his friends had been. As such, his conscience and personal loyalties guided South Africa's foreign policy during a presidency that chose non-alignment not as a least-worst option but as a liberating philosophy.

Remember that Sport and Politics *Do* Mix

'Sport has the power to change the world. It has the power to inspire, it has the power to unite people in a way that little else does. It speaks to youth in a language they understand.'

NELSON MANDELA, SPEAKING AT THE LAUREUS WORLD SPORTS AWARDS, 2000

I t is often said that sport and politics don't mix. Certainly, sport is perhaps at its most wonderful when it rises above the pettiness of everyday life. But to pretend that sport inhabits an entirely different plane of existence is simply a denial of the truth. By its very nature, a sporting contest is one in which one competitor attempts to impose their superiority over another – the very essence of a political act. Throw in the tribalism associated with supporting a particular team, add a dash of nationalism and a generous handful of money in this age of the professional sports-man, and any idealistic hopes of separating sport and politics from one another soon fade.

The canny political operator is thus faced with a simple choice when it comes to sport: can I use it to divide my enemies or to unite people behind my own cause. Mandela realized he had most to gain by following the second route. Ahead of the 1996 African Cup of Nations, the continent's premier football tournament which was hosted by South Africa that year, he spoke publicly of how sport had the innate power to 'overcome old divisions and create the bond of common aspirations'.

Major sporting events have served as important staging posts throughout South Africa's post-apartheid history. Hosting the soccer World Cup in 2010, for instance, brought the nation a chance to show the world just how far it had come in the sixteen years since Mandela was elected president. But without doubt the most significant sporting moment – and one which Mandela manipulated quite brilliantly – happened only a year into his presidency.

THE 1995 RUGBY WORLD CUP

'A flower that blooms in adversity
is the most beautiful and
rare of all.'

FRANÇOIS PIENAAR

For many in South Africa, rugby union has traditionally been much more than a mere leisure pursuit. If rugby is a quasi-religion in Wales and New Zealand, it is no less so in South Africa. Each time fifteen players – tough men stereotypically defined by hard lives lived on the veldt – take to the pitch in those famous green and gold shirts emblazoned with the springbok (the gazelle that serves as the emblem of the team), they carry with them the hopes and expectations of millions of people. However, those interested millions were historically almost exclusively white.

From the 1960s onwards, the nation was subject to assorted cultural and sporting boycotts. The rugby team did continue to tour until 1981 and received touring teams even later than that, but these occasions were often mired in controversy. In 1986, for instance, the British and Irish Lions cancelled a proposed test match series and South Africa was not invited to either of the first two Rugby World Cups in 1987 and 1991.

By 1993, though, it was emerging from its international isolation and two years later it was not only participating in the Rugby World Cup but hosting it. If the white population was filled with excitement at the prospect, most blacks were at best apathetic and more commonly actively willed the team's failure. Rugby was so emblematic of apartheid that there was a tradition of blacks attending matches (in the black-only pens included in certain stadiums) for the express purpose of cheering on the opposition.

While most continued to see the sport as a symbol of the divisions that existed in the nation, Mandela nonetheless saw an opportunity for rapprochement. In the year before the World Cup, Mandela – by then newly installed as President

– summoned the captain of the Springbok team, François Pienaar, to a meeting.

Pienaar, one of four sons from a working-class Afrikaner family, was blonde, strapping and steely-eyed. He might have been specially designed to encapsulate the Springbok ethos in physical form. Yet, he turned out to be the perfect partner in an enterprise aimed at uniting the 'Rainbow Nation' in front of the world. He rose to Mandela's challenge with aplomb and seized his opportunity to play a part in the ushering in of a new era.

Come the tournament, the South African team played its way through some tricky games, defeating France in the semi-final to set up a final appearance against those perennial giants of world rugby, New Zealand. Extraordinarily, by that stage the Springboks were garnering support that transcended racial boundaries. Mandela had called for the entire nation to back the team. The players and the game's administrators played their part too; the squad waged their cup campaign under the slogan 'One Team, One Country' and before each match the players emotionally belted out the newly instituted national anthem, 'Nkosi Sikelel' iAfrika' (God Bless Africa) – a song that until recently had been a hymn of black resistance. Crucially, there was also a black player on the team that the majority of the nation could get behind, a flying winger by the name of Chester Williams.

The final was played at Ellis Park Stadium in Cape Town in front of a 60,000 full house. Ahead of the contest, Mandela marched onto the pitch to greet the players. He wore the Springbok shirt, thus effectively donning the uniform of the old enemy. For a moment the crowd was not sure how to react. Then a rousing chorus of 'Nel-son! Nel-son!' went up.

In a closely fought match – and with several of the New Zealand team apparently having mysteriously contracted food poisoning in the days leading up to the final – South Africa emerged victorious, winning by three points after extra time. Mandela returned to present the trophy, still wearing the national shirt along with a Springbok baseball cap. Presenting the Webb Ellis Cup to Pienaar, Mandela said, 'François, thank you for what you have done for our country.' Pienaar looked him in the eye and responded, 'No, Mr President. Thank you for what you have done.'

A stadium roared and a nation rejoiced. And if anyone doubted that this was a story worthy of a Hollywood movie, it was turned into just that in the 2009 movie, *Invictus*. It was another notable triumph, too, for Mandela's will in adversity. As we have seen elsewhere in this book, he was a man who recognized both the power of sport and of dress. Here, he combined the two to astonishing effect. While the occasion did not mark the end of South Africa's problems, it gave real hope that they may be overcome in the long term. A bastion of apartheid enmity had been reconfigured as a symbol of national unity.

In a 2003 BBC documentary, *Mandela: The Living Legend*, the former president reflected on the impact of the episode: 'The cumulative effect was to allay the fears of the whites and also, by the way, of the blacks because there were many who said, "well this old man is selling out" and who booed me when I said "let us now support rugby, let's regard these boys as our boys".'

Know When
to Step Back

'I welcome the possibility of revelling in obscurity
as I am going to do when I step down.'

NELSON MANDELA, 1999

Twentieth-century Africa was littered with leaders who came to power on a wave of enthusiasm, only to vastly outstay their welcome. Among a long list, we might think of Sekou Toure's violent dictatorship in Guinea from 1958–84, Idi Amin's reign of terror in Uganda in the 1970s or Robert Mugabe's systematic running down of the economy and suppression of opposition in Zimbabwe since 1980.

Mandela was never in danger of following their path. If anything, there was a sense that he removed himself from frontline politics when he still had a job to do. Better surely, though, to leave with his reputation intact rather than undermine the achievements he had taken decades to put into place by hanging on too long. If it takes special attributes to seize and wield power, relinquishing control requires them no less so.

Mandela handed over power in 1999 after a single term in office. It was an act of restraint celebrated in 2013 by no lesser figure than the US President, Barack Obama:

George Washington is admired because after two terms he said, 'Enough, I'm going back to being a citizen.' There were no term limits, but he said, 'I'm a citizen. I served my time. And it's time for the next person, because that's what democracy is about.' And Mandela similarly was able to recognize that, despite how revered he was, that part of this transition process was greater than one person.

Mandela had resigned as ANC President in 1997 with a warning against complacency. He was in his eightieth year and the opportunity to cede power seemed positively to delight him. He told the party:

The time has come to hand over the baton. And I personally relish the moment when my fellow veterans and I shall be able to observe from near and judge from afar. As 1999 approaches, I will endeavour as State President to delegate more and more responsibility, so as to ensure a smooth transition to the new Presidency. Thus I will be able to have that opportunity in my last years to spoil my grandchildren and try in various ways to assist all South African children, especially those who have been the hapless victims of a system that did not care.

His retirement was far from traditional, though, and there was no sign that he was taking the opportunity to put up his feet. Indeed, it took a stark deterioration in his health to prompt him in 2004 to announce his 'retirement from retirement' and a more complete withdrawal from public life. Even then, his statement attested to a man still full of good humour and spirit, going out on a high:

I am not here to announce any fair departures. And in any case, my family and advisors have warned me not to tell my favourite story about arriving at heaven's door, knocking, providing my name and being sent to the other place. Apparently that story makes too many people morose!

Secure Your Legacy

'I would like it to be said that, "Here lies a man who has done his duty on earth".'

NELSON MANDELA IN MSBC DOCUMENTARY, *HEADLINERS AND LEGENDS*, 2006

Having lost his father at a young age and suffered through the premature deaths of many friends and even his own children, it is hardly a surprise that Mandela gave thought to the nature of mortality. 'It is a fact of the human condition,' he told the US Congress in 1990, 'that each shall, like a meteor – a mere brief passing moment in time and space – flit across the human stage and pass out of existence. Even the golden lads and lasses, as much as the chimney sweepers, come, and tomorrow are no more.'

There is no doubt that Mandela's name will echo through the centuries and would have done so from the moment he left prison in 1990 regardless of whatever else followed. The evidence of his impact is burned into the fabric of South Africa: as of 2012 there were some twenty million South Africans who had never lived under the apartheid system.

But there was little chance that Mandela would ever rest on his laurels and in retirement he continued to campaign on social issues. At every opportunity, he promoted 'global co-operation and an uncompromising multilateral approach' as our best hope of addressing inequality and argued that peace is essential to human development. In 2003 he launched outspoken attacks on US President George W. Bush and the UK Prime Minister, Tony Blair, for going to war in Iraq and cited America's history of 'global atrocities'. At the opening of the Oprah Winfrey Leadership Academy in 2007, when Mandela was well into his late eighties, the flame for social justice was still strongly in evidence:

> It can be said that there are four basic and primary things that the mass of people in a society wish for: to live in a safe environment, to be able to work and provide for themselves, to have access to good public health and to have sound educational opportunities for their children. Currently we as a society may be struggling in each of those four areas, but we must remain confident that with the personal commitment of each and every one of us we can and will overcome the obstacles towards development.

But he did not rely on rhetoric alone to make a difference. He took many practical steps to secure his legacy too. Notably, he threw himself into the fight against AIDS with an energy he had not been able to give to the issue while in office. It was a struggle given particular pertinence with the death of his son, Makgatho, from the disease in 2005. However, it was also an uphill battle thanks to the widespread suspicion and ignorance surrounding the illness. Thabo Mbeki,

Mandela's successor as President, hardly helped matters by refusing the medical consensus that AIDS is a viral disease that may be treated with (admittedly expensive) antiretroviral drugs. Instead, he insisted it was caused by poverty, bad diet and a collapse of the immune system resulting from general ill health.

As of 2008, South Africa had some 5.5 million people diagnosed with HIV/AIDS, equating to just under a fifth of the adult population. It is a fight that was never going to be won in Mandela's lifetime. His name, though, will carry on the struggle through the work of the Nelson Mandela Foundation. Established in 1999, the not-for-profit Foundation focuses on the areas of HIV/AIDS, school building and rural development. Since 2006, its core work has been carried out under the aegis of the Nelson Mandela Centre of Memory and it also plays a key role in administering the Nelson Mandela International Day, which was first declared by the UN in 2009. Held on Mandela's birthday, 18 July, Mandela Day aims to inspire individuals to carry out activities such as voluntary work to bring about positive change in the world.

The Foundation has two major sister organizations, the Nelson Mandela Children's Fund (established 1995) and the Mandela Rhodes Foundation (established 2002). The former was in part funded by an endowment of a third of the presidential salary, which Mandela donated for five years. Today it provides assistance to South Africans aged up to twenty-two who are afflicted by homelessness, poverty and AIDS (either directly or as a result of being orphaned) and those living in child-headed households.

The Mandela Rhodes Foundation, meanwhile, joins Mandela's name in an unlikely alliance with Cecil Rhodes, one of the architects of South African colonialism. It seeks to build 'exceptional leadership in Africa' by administering scholarships to African students showing both academic and leadership potential with the long-term aim of developing a network of leaders across the continent. Alongside these three major bodies, there are also a host of supplementary organizations including the 46664 Campaign, the Nelson Mandela Children's Hospital Trust, the Nelson Mandela Museum and the Robben Island Museum.

At his eightieth birthday party, Mandela said: 'One of the advantages of old age is that people respect you just because of your grey hair and say all manner of nice things about you that are not based on who you really are.' The truth, though, is that few people alive today have done more to make an enduring difference to the world.

Trust in Youth

'It is the task of a new generation to lead
and take responsibility; ours has done as
well as it could in its time.'

NELSON MANDELA AT THE LAUNCH
OF THE 2009 ANC MANIFESTO

M andela was an old man when he finished his career as President and even older when he took a significant step back from frontline activism. However, his eagerness to carry on contributing should not be read as a lack of faith in those following after him. He was, in fact, an enthusiastic advocate for youth in general and for the hope and energy that comes with the young.

Just as he sought to make a positive mark on the world, so he understood the need for each new generation to do so. Conversely, he long warned those nearer his own vintage of the dangers of succumbing to complacency and weariness. At an awards ceremony in 1994, he said: 'There can be no process more important for the future of South Africa than the realization of the potential of our youth.' It was a message he reiterated to a global audience at his ninetieth birthday concert for the 46664 project, held in London in 2008. 'We say tonight, after nearly ninety years of life,' he told the adoring crowd, 'it is time for new hands to lift the burdens. It is in your hands now.'

Aware of the part education has played in his own life, Mandela made support for the education of the young one of his top priorities. The importance of education was an argument he was making as long ago as 1953. In that year's 'No Easy Walk to Freedom' speech, he echoed the principles laid out in the Universal Declaration of Human Rights that everyone has the right to education. By 1969 he was telling his son in a letter:

> The issues that agitate humanity today call for trained minds and the man who is deficient in this respect is crippled because he is not in possession of the tools and equipment necessary to ensure success and victory in the service of country and people.

He subsequently spoke of how nothing less than the soul of a nation is revealed through the way it treats its children, arguing that a civilized society is one that provides all its young with an adequate education. 'Children of today are the leaders of tomorrow,' he said in 1990, 'and education is a very important weapon to prepare children for their future roles as leaders of the community.'

With this in mind, he launched the Nelson Mandela Institute for Education and Rural Development in 2007, an organization that strives to address the education crisis confronting vast swathes of rural Africa by working directly with rural teachers, children and parents. At the organization's foundation ceremony, he noted:

There can be no contentment for any of us when there are children, millions of children, who do not receive an education that provides them with dignity and honour and allows them to live their lives to the full. It is not beyond our power to create a world in which all children have access to a good education. Those who do not believe this have small imaginations.

As his life neared its end, Mandela did not struggle to yield power to others. He did, though, seek to make sure that those who follow him are as well-equipped as they may be to do the best job. That is surely the ultimate legacy.

THE ELDERS

While Mandela sought to encourage youth to take on the challenges that South Africa and the world at large faces today, the Elders is perhaps his way of reminding the young that the old carry with them a wealth of knowledge and experience that is neglected at our collective peril.

The Elders is a group of 'independent global leaders working together for peace and human rights' which Mandela formally launched in Johannesburg in 2007. It was the culmination of a process that had begun with an informal conversation with the entrepreneur, Richard

Branson, and the musician, Peter Gabriel, and plugged into Mandela's enduring respect for the Thembu elders whom he watched exchange ideas and wisdom in his childhood. As our world becomes a 'global village', the time seemed right to see if a group of elders could exert similar influence on the worldwide scale.

To qualify for membership, an elder must no longer hold public office and must be independent of any national government or other vested interest. Furthermore, their careers should have won them international standing and trust. They must also have a reputation for integrity and believe in the principles of inclusive, progressive leadership.

The group seeks to solve problems by two main means: by raising public awareness and by using private influence. The members meet twice a year to discuss activities, select specific areas on which to focus and plan strategy. All decisions are taken on the basis of consensus.

The list of members in 2013 included some of the giants of humanitarianism, with experience going back many decades. They included:

- Nelson Mandela (Founder and Honorary Elder)
- Martti Ahtisaari (former Finnish president and Nobel Peace laureate)

- ▶ Kofi Annan (former Secretary-General of the United Nations and Nobel Peace laureate)
- ▶ Ela Bhatt (founder of the Self-Employed Women's Association of India)
- ▶ Lakhdar Brahimi (former Algerian freedom-fighter and Foreign Minister, as well as a UN diplomat)
- ▶ Gro Harlem Brundtland (former premier of Norway and the first woman to hold that post)
- ▶ Fernando Henrique Cardoso (former president of Brazil)
- ▶ Jimmy Carter (former US president and Nobel Peace laureate)
- ▶ Hina Jilani (Pakistani lawyer and human rights campaigner)
- ▶ Graça Machel (Mandela's wife, see page 164)
- ▶ Mary Robinson (former president of Ireland and UN High Commissioner for Human Rights)
- ▶ Archbishop Desmond Tutu (Honorary Elder)
- ▶ Ernesto Zedillo (former president of Mexico)

In an address to the group in 2008, Mandela said:

I am proud to be here, at this ground-breaking first meeting of the Global Elders. As I have said, I am trying to take my retirement seriously and, though I will not be able to participate in the really exciting part of the work, analysing problems, seeking solutions, searching out partners, I will be with you in spirit.

Quotes About Mandela

'It's a blessing that South Africa has a man
like Nelson Mandela.'

ARCHBISHOP DESMOND TUTU

'Nelson Mandela is, for me, the single statesman
in the world. The single statesman, in that literal
sense, who is not solving all his problems
with guns. It's truly unbelievable.'

TONI MORRISON

'May Nelson Mandela's life of service to others and
his unwavering commitment to equality, reconciliation,
and human dignity continue to be a beacon for
each future generation seeking a more just
and prosperous world.'

BARACK OBAMA

Quotes About Mandela

'He cannot help magnetising a crowd: he is
commanding with a tall, handsome bearing; trusts and
is trusted by the youth, for their impatience reflects his
own; appealing to the women. He is dedicated and
fearless. He is the born mass leader.'

OLIVER TAMBO

'Mandela didn't give someone else the permission to
define his life, his worth, and his tomorrows. If you have
lost a bunch of yesterdays, welcome to the human race.
You still don't have to give anybody your tomorrows.
That's advice we should all take to heart and try to
follow. Even for Mandela it was sometimes easier to say
than do, but with discipline and determination, he did it.'

BILL CLINTON

'Yes, Mandela's day is done, yet we, his inheritors,
will open the gates wider for reconciliation, and we
will respond generously to the cries of Blacks
and Whites, Asians, Hispanics, the poor
who live piteously on the floor of our planet.'

MAYA ANGELOU, *HIS DAY IS DONE*

'That's the thing, you know, he's inscrutable.
He's the coolest man that I have ever
come across. Unflappable.'

AHMED KATHRADA

Selected
Bibliography

Boehmer, Elleke, *Nelson Mandela: A Very Short Introduction*, OUP (2008)

Lodge, Tom, *Mandela: A Critical Life*, OUP (2007)

Mandela, Nelson, *Conversations with Myself*, Macmillan (2010)

Mandela, Nelson, *Long Walk to Freedom*, Abacus (1994)

Mandela, Nelson, *Nelson Mandela By Himself: The Authorised Book of Quotations*, Macmillan (2011)

Mandela, Nelson, *Nelson Mandela's Favorite African Folktales*, W. W. Norton & Co (2008)

Meer, Fatima, *Higher Than Hope: A Biography of Nelson Mandela*, Penguin Books (1990)

Meredith, Martin, *Mandela: A Biography*, Simon & Schuster (2010)

Ndoyiya, Xoliswa & Trapido, Anna, *Ukutya Kwasekhaya: Tastes from Nelson Mandela's Kitchen*, Anna Real African Publishers Pty Ltd (2011)

Sampson, Anthony, *Mandela: The Authorised Biography*, HarperPress (2011)

Selected Bibliography

Stengel, Richard, *Nelson Mandela: Portrait of an Extraordinary Man*, Virgin Books (2012)

Trapido, Anna, *Freedom: The Story of Food in the Life of Nelson Mandela*, Jacana Media (Pty) Ltd (2008)

Woods, Donald, *Rainbow Nation Revisited: South Africa's Decade of Democracy*, Andre Deutsch (2004)